The Music
of
Time

The Music
of
Time

WORDS AND MUSIC AND
SPIRITUAL FRIENDSHIP

John S. Dunne

University of Notre Dame Press
NOTRE DAME AND LONDON

Copyright 1996 by
University of Notre Dame Press
Notre Dame, IN 46556
All rights reserved

Book design by Wendy Torrey McMillen
Set in 11/14 Janson by Books International
Printed and bound by Edwards Brothers, Inc.

Manufactured in the United States of America

Library of Congress Cataloging-in-Publication Data

Dunne, John S., 1929–
    The music of time : words and music and spiritual
friendship / John S. Dunne.
        p.   cm.
    Includes bibliographical references and index.
    ISBN 0-268-01423-x (alk. paper)
    1. Spiritual life—Catholic authors.   2. Dunne, John S.,
1929–   3. Christian literature—Authorship.   4. Music—
Religious aspects—Christianity.   5. Friendship—Religious
aspects—Christianity.
    I. Title
    BX2350.2.D87   1996
    248—dc20   95-47364
                                                        CIP

The paper used in this publication meets the minimum
requirements of the American National Standard for Information
Sciences—Permanance of Paper for Printed Library Materials,
ANSI z39.48-1984.

Contents

v

vi | Contents

Preface

I have always been haunted by "the road not taken," as Robert Frost called it, the road in life I could have taken and didn't. But in these last years I have come to believe that the road not taken can rejoin the road taken in life. Let me rework the poem then.

Two roads once diverged for me, one the solitary way of the spiritual adventure and the other the way of companionship in life, and I—I took the solitary way. Again, two roads once diverged for me, one the way of words and the other the way of music, and I chose the way of words as the way in which I felt stronger—it was like choosing between my right hand and my left hand. Now I have come to a meeting of the ways where all of them rejoin. I am composing again, something I did as a teenager, and I can feel a surge of new life as the way of words and the way of music come together. But I find something even more unexpected, the solitary way of the spiritual adventure and the way of human companionship are coming together too, in the way of spiritual friendship.

"Words and Music and Spiritual Friendship," that is my subtitle and describes the way I am taking here, and this book contains my "waymarkings." The integral way I have come to is an ancient way—I can see it in Saint Augustine retiring with his friends to the country and writing dialogues about "music," meaning by that term both music and poetry. I find, however, the ways I have taken are more accessible to me than the ways I have not taken, the way of words more than the way of music, the solitary way of the spiritual adventure more than the way of spiritual friendship. In taking the ways I have not taken I am becoming whole, using my left hand as well as my right, but I am coming up against my own shadow, my own unlived life. Among the lyrics I composed while writing this book and included here are the lyrics of a "Shadow Dance":

> I leap over
> my own shadow
> and it leaps on
> into mystery.

That is what I am doing here, trying to leap over my own shadow while it leaps on into mystery. When you try to leap over your own shadow, it always leaps on ahead of you.

There is an element of mystery in our lives, an element of the unknown, that "shows itself and at the same time withdraws." We come upon it especially when we come upon our own shadow, our own unlived life. There is a music of time, an ebb and flow in our lives and in our relationships with one another, as mystery shows itself and withdraws. It is like the ebb and flow of the tide. In fact, "tide" is an old word for time, and the ebb and flow of human affairs was once linked with "the music of the spheres," just as the ebb and flow of the tide can be linked with the gravitation of the moon. Now, instead of "the music of the spheres," we might be inclined to speak rather of "the music of chance." But calling it simply "the music of time," I want to suggest there is more than chance in our lives and in our encounters with one another. We can salvage from the flow of time the typical shapes of our longing, and we can recognize in memory the deserted places of our heart. So memory can become for us a theatre-in-the-round where we see "a dance to the music of time."[1]

Naming this book *The Music of Time*, I am thinking of time as "a changing image of eternity," Plato's definition, and seeing the ebb and flow as that of eternity in time. The eternal in us comes to light in words and music and spiritual friendship. It is "the mystery of your loneliness,"[2] as Shakespeare calls it in *All's Well That Ends Well*, and that is our hope in life, I believe, that somehow the longing in our loneliness will be fulfilled and all will be well. Helena in that play is in love with Bertram and that is all the mystery of her loneliness, but the longing in our loneliness goes deep and unabated in our finite loves. It is our taste, our foretaste, our aftertaste of a love that is infinite. "The love is from God and of God and towards God,"[3] the old Bedouin said to Lawrence of Arabia. We love with a love we do not know, I believe, and longing is love as we know it, and our longing can become for us the love of God. That is the mystery of our loneliness, I want to say, showing itself and at the same time withdrawing in our finite loves. It shows itself in our loves and hides itself in our loneliness. Or should I say rather it shows itself in our loneliness and hides itself in our loves?

"All's well that ends well,"[4] the title of the play, becomes a line of Helena's, expressing her hope of fulfilment in love. I think of the Helena in love also in *A Midsummer Night's Dream* and her phrase "Love's mind" that I used as the title of my last book. What can I know of love? That was the question I was asking about "Love's mind." What may I hope of love? That is the question I am asking about "All's well that ends well." I find an answer in Grimm's saying, "One human heart goes out to another, undeterred by what lies between."[5] I find another kind of answer in the prayer, "Keep me friendly to myself, keep me gentle in disappointment."[6] There is a going out to another in "passing over," as I call it, entering sympathetically into the life and thought of another, and then there is a "coming back" to my own life. That has been my method on the way of words. I see the ebb and flow of mystery here, the flow in the passing over, the ebb in the coming back.

If I use the method of passing over also in music, I find myself imagining musical expressions of love and loneliness, imagining the simple African love song,

I walk alone,

as Jazz, Blues, Soul, Country, Rock, and Metal. Passing over into these ways of "music as a state of being," I am experimenting with the willingness and the unwillingness to walk alone, the willingness that welcomes companionship and the unwillingness that requires companionship. Coming back to myself and to my own sense of life as a journey with God, I find "He that lives in hope danceth without musick,"[7] as George Herbert says. I am living in hope, I am dancing without music, but if I seek musical expression of such a hope, I find it in "music as symbolic form," for instance in Mozart's *Ave Verum*, where there is a sense of "God with us." The willingness to walk alone and the hope of being unalone go together, it seems, like the willingness to die and the hope to live. Giving expression to willing hope is like putting words to songs that are without words, putting music to dance that is without music. It is giving expression to "the singing timelessness of the heart."

If I bring the method of passing over also to spiritual friendship, I find there too the ebb and flow, the flow of intimacy and passing over, the ebb of distance and coming back to myself. But I can see how the ebb and flow is linked with the ins and outs, the days and nights of the spiritual adventure, the ebb with the night of spiritual desolation, the flow with the day of spiritual consolation. I can see too how the ebb and flow comes about without my choosing. And in the spiritual night of desolation I can see a new meaning in the song "I walk alone." The love song becomes a mystical song of the love of God. For the ebb and flow is really that of the mystery that shows and withdraws in the spiritual adventure itself.

If I go with the ebb and flow, passing over with the flow and coming back with the ebb, I follow the lead of the mystery, I walk alone and unalone. I find I cannot "pluck out the heart of my mystery,"[8] as Hamlet says, but can only wait on its showing and withdrawing, following its elusive light like sea fire on a journey like that of Mossy and Tangle in "The Golden Key" where

> if you lose each other,
> do not be afraid, go on and on,

but where the light is as kindly as in the story of Antonio and Cordolina in "The Church of the Poor Devil,"

> O light,
> shine on

divided heart,
and wandering eye,
and my poor devil's cry!

I have included all these lyrics of mine at the end in an appendix called "Lyric Theatre." I have not included the music I composed for them: there are fragments of Gregorian chant in the melodies, and there is a tendency to combine diatonic and what Nicolas Slonimsky calls "pandiatonic" harmony in the piano accompaniment. My thanks go to those who worked with me in putting on "The Church of the Poor Devil" (November 23, 1993), Karen Wonder, the soprano; Patrick Birge, the tenor; and Lisa DeBoer the dancer and choreographer, and to those who worked with me in putting on "The Golden Key" (April 4, 1995), Brenda Wonder, the soprano; Maura Pheney, the alto; Jeffrey Graham, the tenor; James Foster, the baritone and narrator; and Kathryn Turner, the dancer and choreographer, and to Sister Joris Binder, the sponsor of both performances in Pasquerilla East at Notre Dame. My thanks go also to Kristen Sullivan, who sang some of these songs and some from my earlier song cycle "Ayasofya" after a lecture I gave called "The Music of Time" at Maryknoll in New York (October 27, 1994). I was at the piano in all these performances, but in composing and playing all these song and dance cycles I felt I was learning something, if not to leap over my own shadow, at least to walk the road not taken.

The Music of Time

The Road goes ever on and on.

—J. R. R. Tolkien

There are roads in life that dead-end, roads where the limits of the possible in love and work are soon exhausted, and there are roads where life seems inexhaustible, roads that go ever on and on. This last is the title and the theme song of a song cycle by Tolkien, *The Road Goes Ever On*.[1] What is it that enables a road to go on and not dead-end?

We love with a love we do not know, I believe, a love we do not fully understand, and so we live a life we do not fully understand, and when we realize this, we find ourselves on a road that goes ever on and on into the unknown. I think of an old man I heard of recently who loved books and who lived in a motel room surrounded by thousands of books he had collected, hoping to give them to a small town that had no public library. An earthquake came and all his books fell on him, and firefighters digging through the books saw his foot under the tumble. When he was carried to a hospital and came to consciousness, he asked for a glass of orange juice and a book to read.[2] When I saw his face in photographs, the very gentle face of an eighty-seven-year-old man, I thought of the words in *Shadowlands*, the screenplay about C. S.

Lewis, "We read to know that we are not alone."³ The old man's love of books is like all our love, I thought. It expresses the longing in the deep loneliness of the human condition, the longing "to know that we are not alone."

I think of the love of music as well as the love of words. I had a dream once in which I heard Schubert play five piano pieces. When he came to the last one he smiled and said, "This one is called Inner Music for the Piano." (I learned afterwards that he does indeed have a composition called "Five Piano Pieces," perhaps an unfinished sonata, and the fifth piece has the unusual tempo marking *Allegro patetico*, as if to say "joyful sorrowful").⁴ I wonder if there is a music in us, an inner music, not just emotion, not just cognition, but the ebb and flow of our inner life of knowing and loving, an inner tide, an inner time that resonates with music. I wonder if making music is a way of being unalone, of making our inner music heard, and if listening is a way of knowing that we are not alone.

I think also of friendship and of something Helen Luke once said, "I believe friendship is the highest thing," the highest of all our loves I think she meant, if we do not include the love of God, but then the love of God too can take the form of a friendship with God. There is an ebb and flow of friendship that is perhaps the very ebb and flow of our inner life of knowing and loving. Speaking of the "constancy" of friendship, a friend of mine wrote "I find it much easier, actually, to remove myself at times, to 'disappear' somewhere behind the distance that separates me from that handful of people whom I do care about deeply. And then the love is always there to draw me back again."

Our longing to be unalone, to know that we are not alone, ebbs and flows, I can see, and there is a near and a far in our relationship with one another, and even in our relationship with God. There is an intimacy and a distance, an intimacy in distance, a distance in intimacy, that keeps the relationship ebbing and flowing and gives us the sense of being on a road that goes "ever on and on." If there were just intimacy, if there were just distance, the road would dead-end.

There is an ebb and flow, a near and far, in our relation with the unknown in life, the mystery of life. "That which shows itself and at the same time withdraws is the essential trait of what we call the mystery,"[5] Heidegger says. The unknown, the mystery, shows itself and withdraws in words and in music and in friendship, or put the other way around, our loving and our knowing ebbs and flows. When our love is flowing, the mystery seems to be showing itself, and we seem to be knowing, and when our love is ebbing, the mystery seems to be withdrawing, and we seem to be left in a darkness of unknowing. Still, the withdrawing evokes our longing and causes the flowing to begin all over again. So we are led along the road by an elusive light, the light of mystery, that shows and withdraws and leads us on and on.

What counts in life, it seems, is our relationship to the mystery. This came home to me as an insight one night after seeing Jean Vanier honored for his work with the mentally handicapped.[6] The day before I had attended a children's piano recital, and the two events seemed to converge. I had just read something Einstein said a month before he died, after spending the last years of his life in a vain search for an alternative to the quantum theory, convinced as he was that "God does not play dice." Realizing he had not succeeded, he said "However that may be, Lessing's comforting word stays with us: the aspiration to truth is more precious than its assured possession."[7] Those words seemed to me to name what I was learning from listening to the children's recital and then listening to Jean Vanier's stories of the mentally handicapped. The aspiration to truth is more precious because it is a relationship of love, while the assured possession is a relationship pervaded by illusion. If the truth takes the shape of a mystery that "shows itself and at the same time withdraws," our highest relationship with the truth is one of loving the truth and of knowing that comes of loving.

Knowing that comes of loving is the affirmative way, and knowing that comes of unknowing is the negative way to truth. When I say "unknowing," I mean something like "unlearning." I am thinking of "the cloud of unknowing in the which a soul is oned with God."[8] By unknowing all I think I know of God and of myself, dropping all my preconceived notions of God and of myself, I open the way to knowing that comes of loving. Unknowing is a process of thinking back through time and memory; the knowing that comes of loving, on the other hand, arises in an equal and opposite process of thinking forward into a reality that is greater than ourselves. Thinking back is like breathing in, "thou in me," as my sister says, quoting the Gospel of John, and thinking forward is like breathing out, "I in thee."

Unknowing, when it is separated from knowing that comes of loving, can become a destructive process. Thinking back, *andenken* as Heidegger called it, has become in our times a process of "deconstruction," of unraveling human constructs. If we unlearn all we think we know of God and of ourselves, dropping our preconceived notions, but do not go out in love to the reality that is greater than ourselves, we are left with ourselves. We find ourselves on a road that dead-ends in a "face, seen at the bottom of a deep well,"[9] a face that is our own. If we remain open to the mystery, however, open to knowing that comes of loving, we can see the face at the bottom of the well as a face also of God, as if to say "God dwells in you as you."[10] I learned the formula "God dwells in you as you" from a Hindu friend, and when I asked her what it meant to her, she told me it cuts right through the deep loneliness that separates us from one another. So here again I find the longing that seems to pervade all our love, the longing "to know that we are not alone."

If we follow the longing and let it lead us out into a reality that is greater than ourselves, we find ourselves on a road that does not dead-end but goes ever on and on. Knowing takes reality in, while loving goes out to reality. But when it comes to a reality greater than ourselves, or even to our own reality equal to ourselves, we cannot take it in except insofar as it is already there in us. We go out to reality by "passing over," I call it, entering sympathetically into the lives and thoughts of others, and we take reality in by "coming back" to ourselves, to new insight into our own lives. "Our relation to our fellow human beings is that of prayer," as Kafka says, "our relation to ourselves that of striving."[11] When I read the words of others and let them speak to my heart, I enter into something like prayer where "heart speaks to heart," as if God were speaking to my heart through the words of another and I were communing with God.

If there is a road that does not dead-end, it is "the road of the union of love with God,"[12] as Saint John of the Cross calls it in his *Dark Night of the Soul*, and it is by passing through a dark night of unknowing that we come to loving and to knowing that comes of loving. We seem to be in the midst of a dark night of unknowing in our times. It is an unknowing that is at times willing, as in "deconstruction," at times unwilling, as in "fundamentalism" now arisen in the great religions East and West. And it can seem in this dark night that love is only "the will to love."[13] If we enter the unknowing not only with willingness but also with hope, though, we find ourselves already on "the road of the union of love with God," and each time we pass over to others we take a step with one foot, and each time we come back again to ourselves we take a step with the other foot, catching up with ourselves.

Words and music and friendship leave us alone and un-alone, alone in the ebb that is solitude and unalone in the flow that is communication, and yet we want to be alone as well as "to know that we are not alone." We want both the pleasures of solitude and the pleasures of communication. We want both the ebb and the flow. I see "passing over" in the flow of communication and "coming back" in the ebb of solitude. There is even a metaphor of creation in this ebb and flow, the thought of God creating the world by drawing back, *zimzum* as the Hasidim say, ebbing like the tide and letting us and everything else exist but leaving everywhere the traces of the flow; the Presence (the Shekinah), like tide pools flashing with light. We want both the ebb and the flow; we want to exist, to be separate, even to be alone, and yet we want "the union of love with God" and "to know that we are not alone." The union or reunion, then, is not a unity of being, like that of God before the creation, but a union of loving and knowing.

So if the mystery "shows itself and at the same time withdraws," our heart's desire is not to forestall its withdrawal so much as to follow its elusive light. If I follow its light, I find it withdraws into my memory and into time past and takes me in thought all the way back to the beginning, but then, as I realize the end of thinking back is really the beginning of thinking forward, it leads me forward on many roads of human possibility, showing me roads that dead-end and roads that converge, leading into a road that goes ever on and on. "He used often to say there was only one Road," Tolkien has it in his trilogy, "that it was like a great river: its springs were at every doorstep, and every path was its tributary."[14] Maybe roads that dead-end really dead-end into the road that goes ever on and on.

And if love's road is the one that goes ever on, knowledge of God and of ourselves is something that comes about on love's road, a growing vision. I think of the warning, "Where there is no vision, the people perish."[15] Let us see what vision we can come to by thinking back and thinking forward along love's road. Thinking back, we are asking ourselves the question that is asked in the Gospel of John, "Where do you come from?" And thinking forward, we are asking ourselves the other great question that is asked there, "Where are you going?" Thinking on the road behind and the road ahead, we are able at last to discover where we are now. And that is vision, to be able to see behind and to see ahead, even though it is only to become conscious of the unknown behind and the unknown ahead, to situate ourselves between two unknowns. Like Goethe saying "The Eternal Feminine draws us on,"[16] we can say "The mystery draws us ever on and on."

A Memory Theatre

At wit's end is God.[1]

—proverb

There comes a point in the later years of your life when it seems there is no more hope. It is too late, as it seems, for the fulfilment of your heart's desire in life, too late for love, too late for work. When you have been living with that thought long enough to be on the verge of despair or of desperation, "at wit's end," a thought comes from somewhere else—from God? from the other side of the brain? It is a thought that brings hope where there was no hope, a way where there was no way. It arises out of memory, as it seems, out of the past, though it has to do with hope, with the future.

Say the thought comes of a spiritual friendship, like that of Mossy and Tangle in George MacDonald's story *The Golden Key*. It is like the thought of a happy ending, "And they lived together happily ever after." Only in MacDonald's story it is "And by this time I think they must have got there." That is because a spiritual friendship is a sharing of, a going together on, a spiritual journey and so the happy ending is to "have got there," to come together to the journey's end. A spiritual journey goes on through death and beyond, as in this story, and so too a spiritual friendship is not simply "until death do us part" but embraces life on both sides of death. The law of the spiritual friendship is stated at one point in the story when the Lady of the Forest advises Mossy and Tangle as they set out together, "And if you should lose each other as you go through the—the—I never can remember the name of that country,—do not be afraid, but go on and on."[2] And that does happen in the story, they lose one another in the Valley of Shadows, and Tangle remembers the words of the Lady and goes "on and on."

There is hope in spiritual friendship, hope in life and in life after life. It is the hope of the spiritual adventure itself, but it is more inclusive, as a sharing of life with another person. When I have hope only for myself, there is something in me that despairs. My hope has to include more than myself to be free of despair. Really, to be pure of all despair, it has somehow to include everyone, like Origen's hope of universal reconciliation (*apocatastasis*). There is a willingness to walk alone in that counsel, "if you should lose each other . . . do not be afraid, but go on and on," and yet there is a hope of companionship, of finding one another once again, as Mossy and Tangle do in the end. They find each other and they find others as well, "and beautiful beings of all ages climbed along with them."[3]

"Love is of such a nature that it changes us into the things we love,"[4] Meister Eckhart says. Although I do not become the persons I love, I do acquire the qualities I love in them. Thus when Mossy and Tangle meet again, he sees in her the beauty of the Lady of the Forest and the peace and stillness of the ancient child she has met called the Old Man of the Fire. If I tell my own story in a similar fashion as a story of encounters with other persons, of passing over to them and coming back again to myself, I am telling it as a story of love changing me into the things I love. My memory is a theatre containing images of the things I love, of my own changes, and of the love that changes me. If my memory were organized, it would be what in Shakespeare's time was called "a memory theatre."[5] Let me see if I can organize it and open a theatre of memory and hope.

The Shapes of Longing

"All the enjoyment of love is in the love itself,"[6] according to an ancient saying often quoted in the tradition of spiritual friendship. There is a detachment in love that can make a friendship something spiritual. There is a self-transcendence in passing over to others, and yet there is always a coming back to myself that leaves me in possession of myself but not of others. I have to find in myself the things I love in others, and this leads me back to a vision of things in which "the soul is somehow all things."[7] My memory theatre is a theatre of all things as they exist in the soul. I find them all there in the shapes of my longing, the successive shapes that heart's desire has taken in my life. There are the stories I heard and loved as a child listening to my grandfather on our front porch on summer evenings, and there are those I learned afterwards, reading by myself. There are the songs I heard my mother play on the piano and those I learned to play myself, improvising and learning to read music. And there are the drawings I saw my father make and those I learned to make myself with pencil and ink and watercolor.

Here are three realms, story and song and design. Each story, each song, each design is a shape of longing. I think of Tolkien and his trilogy of story, his song cycle, and his maps and pictures of his imaginary world. All three realms are linked in content and all are pervaded by a nostalgia, a longing for what "was" and for what "is," as Tolkien says, and for what "will ever be."[8] As I think of these realms in my own memory, I can see each one of them has been augmented as life has gone on, and each has undergone a process also of realization. Augmenting them has meant more stories, more songs, more designs. But it has also meant broadening the realm of story to include sayings and all the realm of words, broadening that of song to include dance and all the realm of music, and broadening that of design to include "design by accident" and ultimately "to behold the entire world in one ray of the sun."[9]

Realizing story and song and design has meant asking myself about my own story, my own song, my own world. *What do I see "in one ray of the sun"?* Do I see "light can be both wave and particle"? Do I see "in the splendor of gleaming light the joys of heavenly life"?[10] In fact, I have learned to see in both ways, and so I see an illumining of the mind and a kindling of the heart. When I walk along the shore, I see how the sunlight makes a path of reflection on the water coming to me, following me as I walk to and fro, and when I look at the stars in the night sky, I think of the light traveling thousands of light years to reach my eye, as if an individual were significant after all in so vast a universe. To see the significance of the individual human being is an illumining of the mind and a kindling of the heart. It is to see the significance of every human being and also my own significance. It is to see the importance of every story and of my own story, of every song and of my own song, of every human world and of my own world. "God is spirit,"[11] I can see, and God works by illumining minds and kindling hearts.

If I think of God as spirit, working in my life by illumining my mind and kindling my heart, then every time I come to my wit's end, and that seems to be at regular intervals, I find myself waiting on God to work in my mind and my heart. I wait for an illumining, a kindling, for new light, new fire. I do not look for God to be an item in my memory but to be the "kindly Light" that sets things in my memory glowing. "Images must be charged with affects, and particularly the affect of Love," it is said of images in memory, "for so they have power to penetrate to the core of both the outer and the inner worlds," power to open "the black diamond doors"[12] of the soul. Let me see what happens to the images in my own memory if I open my memory theatre.

"No matter how far back my love memories go, I find it difficult to talk about them," Julia Kristeva says at the beginning of her *Tales of Love*. "They relate to an exaltation beyond eroticism that is as much inordinate happiness as it is pure suffering; both turn words into passion."[13] Including, as I am doing, the love of things as well as the love of persons, the love of words and music, the love of all I see "in one ray of the sun," I find it even truer to say that love memories relate to an exaltation that is beyond eroticism. There are four memories, W. B. Yeats says in *A Vision:* there is the memory of the events of life, the memory of past lives, the memory of ideas, and the memory of moments of exaltation.[14] These "moments of exaltation," as he calls them, are connected with the ideas displayed by the persons of one's life or of past lives. So all four memories are connected. It is the moments of exaltation, of illumining and kindling, that bring the persons and the ideas and the events of memory into the light, though at the same time they "turn words into passion."

Some of these moments of exaltation are moments of "inordinate happiness." Some are moments of "pure suffering." Sometimes the light seems indeed a "kindly Light," sometimes a light that hurts as I am brought face-to-face with the truth of my life. Always, though, there is an exaltation of feeling. When affect is lost, memories fade and the places of memory become a labyrinth, a bewildering maze. "Living in the labyrinth" is how Diana Friel McGowin describes "a personal journey through the maze of Alzheimer's,"[15] a remarkable story, full of courage, by one actually suffering from Alzheimer's disease, undergoing the loss of self that goes with the loss of memory. As more recent memories fade, she returns to childhood memories, still vivid and charged with affect, and she contrives to meet again with people she remembers from childhood, people for whom she still has the vivid feeling of a child. Love, it seems, is the Ariadne's thread that guides her through the labyrinth.

If I let love guide me through the maze of memory, the labyrinth changes into a theatre where the events of my life are reenacted, where life is lived again and persons are met again and ideas are learned again, where all "the four perturbations of the mind,"[16] as Augustine called them, are felt again: desire and gladness and fear and sadness. And yet with love as my guide, I don't simply feel desire and gladness and fear and sadness. What I feel is what Wordsworth, defining poetry, called "emotion recollected in tranquillity."[17] Say I come in memory upon all the ins and outs of a friendship, the desire to be friends, the gladness of having a friend, the fear of losing my friend, the sadness of having lost my friend. It is the recollection of all these emotions in tranquillity that turns the friendship into a spiritual friendship. It is the love that guides me that enables me to "go on and on," to be willing to walk alone and yet hope to meet again. It is the love that guides me that is the real love of spiritual friendship, "such a love as none can part."[18]

What love is this that guides me? It is my heart's longing taking one shape after another, an enthusiasm for stories, an enthusiasm for music, an enthusiasm for what I can see "in one ray of the sun." It is a longing that becomes love by way of friendship, surviving the ins and outs of friendship to become "such a love as none can part." It is a longing, I believe, that turns out to be the love of God, the longing Augustine is speaking of when he says in prayer "our heart is restless until it rests in you."[19] Its restless movement from image to image can take us on a tour of memory, never letting us rest in any one image or become obsessed or possessed by an image and taken thus with violence. "For in a sense the very restlessness of desire," Leo Bersani says in *The Forms of Violence*, "is a guarantee of its curiously mild and pacific nature."[20]

How then does our heart come to rest in God? When Augustine searches for God in his memory, he does not find God among the images, but he ends his search saying "Late have I loved you."[21] If God is the light that illumines my mind and kindles my heart, then God has been there all along, at work in my life, working in my mind and heart, and when I finally come to realize this it seems late. To realize it is to remember God, and to remember is to love God, and to love is to rest in God. Say I am at the point in a friendship where we have lost one another, and I am trying to "go on and on." Remembering God at this point, realizing God has been and is at work, illumining and kindling, I begin to realize "such a love as none can part." It is then that Wisdom seems to speak and say "if you should lose one another . . .

do not be afraid, but go on and on." As I go on and on, the restless movement of my heart continues, but I find rest in the realization that God is at work in my mind and in my heart, leading me through that restless movement, never letting me rest in anything but God.

"Wisdom is repose in light," Joseph Joubert says in his *Notebooks*; "for repose in light can be—tends to be—peace through light," Maurice Blanchot comments, "light that appeases and that gives peace, but repose in light is also repose—deprivation of all external help and impetus—so that nothing comes to disturb, or to pacify, the pure movement of light."[22] If I rest in the light that illumines my mind and kindles my heart, I do find peace through light, I experience the kindliness of the "kindly Light," but I also experience the truth of my own life revealed by the light, a truth that can be hard to bear. There is a truth about my life that comes to light, for instance, in the parting of friends. I am alone in the light, and yet I have the company of the light.

If I think of the inner light not only as Light Within but as Christ Within, as Quakers do, then the inner light seems to speak to my loneliness and I seem to have very real and personal company as I walk through my memory. Calling the inner light the Christ Within, I think of Christ in the Gospel of John and the language there of life and light and love. Christ is the life of my soul, according to this language, the light that illumines my mind, the love that kindles my heart. I think also of the vision in John of coming from God and returning to God, and I think of the questions "Where do you come from?" and "Where are you going?" If I ask those questions of the persons of my life, I see their exits and their entrances on the stage of my memory theatre, and if I ask myself those questions I come to the boundaries of my memory, thinking back to birth and forward to death (*memento mori*). But if I ask those questions of the Christ Within, like Pilate asking "Where do you come from?" and Peter asking "Where are you going?" I am asking questions that arise "at wit's end," and I come to a vision of coming from God and returning to God.

Such a vision expresses "the transcendence of longing," as Theodor Adorno calls it, how longing always goes beyond its finite object and so, I would say, returns to God, as if coming from God and going to God. Such a vision or such a principle as "the transcendence of longing" can organize my memory, especially if I think of the images in memory as shapes of longing. It is a principle that accounts for many things in my memory. If I have made another person the object of my longing, for instance, or the other has made me the object, our relationship will not be lasting, for my longing will go beyond the other and the other's beyond me. It is only by sharing the longing with one another, as in a spiritual friendship, and sharing the adventure it leads us on, that our relationship can last, as longing passes from one shape to another.

Still, "Longing is not extinguished in the images," Adorno says of the shapes of longing, "but survives in them just as it emanates from them. By the strength of the immanence of their content, the transcendence of longing is achieved."[23] All my enthusiasms are still alive in my memory, that is, my love of stories and the stories I have loved, my love of music and the songs I have loved, my love of all I have seen "in one ray of the sun." All my loves and friendships are still alive there too, even the ones that have not been lasting. What is there in recollection is the "emotion recollected in tranquillity." My heart's longing is not extinguished in them but survives in them and emanates from them, as Adorno says, and it is by their presence in my memory, "by the strength of the immanence of their content," that my heart's longing goes on, "the transcendence of longing is achieved." If they were wiped out of my memory, I would have to start over.

"Images remember,"[24] as Michael Perlman says. There are the images of persons I keep in my heart, not only those who are near but also those who are far away, not only the living but also the dead, as if two worlds were really one, as they are in stories, as if we did live on both sides of death. There are the images of things I personify, elemental beings I envision as persons, like the Old Man of the Sea, the Old Man of the Earth, and the Old Man of the Fire in *The Golden Key*, where figure and ground are reversed, where what is ground to the human figure becomes itself a figure—it is like having an I-and-thou relationship with a tree, like a friend of mine who used to talk with trees. And there is the image of myself as more than a sum of my experiences, as a whole that is more than a sum of parts—it is an image of the human being as a mystery. All of these images remember someone or something, as if memory were filled with images rather than facts, as if it were true to say as the novelist Joao Ubaldo Ribeiro does, "there are no facts, there are only stories."[25]

Songs remember too, melodies like those of plainsong that are able to bring another world to mind and to make me remember the other world while I am living in this world, again as if the two worlds were really one. There are songs too where figure and ground are reversed, songs addressing ground as if it were figure, songs to the inner light such as "Lead, Kindly Light," songs to divine love such as "Love bade me welcome," and all mystical songs where I sing to the ground of my life as to a person. And there are songs, if I may call them that, and dances too that I hear when I listen to my inner wholeness, a wholeness that is more than a sum of parts, and I hear the sea of human longing or the sea of divine love—"We listen to our inmost selves," as Martin Buber says, "and we do not know which sea we hear murmuring."[26] To sing and to listen, to be a singing listener, a listening singer is to remember.

And there is all I remember when I see "one ray of the sun," the light of this world and the light of the other world, here too as if the two worlds were really one. I see a luminous human figure against a dark ground, as if an individual human being were significant in a vast and mysterious universe, then again a dark figure like a shadow or a silhouette against a luminous ground, as if life and light and love were at the heart of the universe. I see a universe that is more than a sum of parts, a human being too that is more than a sum of parts, a whole within a whole, a microcosm within a macrocosm. I think of George Crumb's composition *Makrokosmos* where the visual signs of the Zodiac become music and music in score becomes spiral and circular design. If my memory theatre were to be like one of the Renaissance, it might be organized around a set of symbols like these, like the chapter room of an abbey I visited where the signs of the Zodiac are shown in panels on the ceiling along with scenes of the creation of the world, and the monastic rule is exhibited in symbols and words in leaded glass windows along the walls.[27]

Yet it is "the transcendence of longing" rather than a set of symbols that underlies these principles I am using about two worlds, about figure and ground, and about the whole and a sum of parts. My longing goes beyond one world to another, beyond figure to ground, beyond a sum of parts to the whole. It is the transcendence of longing that carries me also from one realm to another, from story to song to design and back. The passageways in my memory theatre are carved out by my longing. It is by coming into touch with my heart and its longing that I am able to remember, and that the images of memory come alive as shapes of longing, and that the passageways of memory open up before me. It is longing that gives me both energy and direction. So my memory is being organized as if it were a continuum rather than a set of discrete units. It is as though I could enter my memory and always find new things rather than simply the set of things I have consciously placed there.

Say in a moment of acute loneliness I ask myself about my own life story, "Where do you come from?" and "Where are you going?" Asking myself that "at wit's end" is like asking it of the inner light at work in my life. I begin to see Meister Eckhart's point, that what is said of Christ can be said also of us. I begin to see how the basic Christian symbols in my memory, those of coming from God and returning to God, apply not only to Christ but also to us, how it belongs not only to life and light and love to come from God and return to God but it belongs also to loneliness. It is as if I remembered something about my own life, my own birth and death, that I never knew. It is as if my loneliness were to be realized in life and light and love. I have to ask for its realization, "Let my heart be according to your heart!"

If my story is of loneliness to be realized in life and light and love, my song is my prayer for its realization, and if "heart speaks to heart" in my prayer, I can hope my prayer is itself already a beginning of realization. My loneliness is acute because of the ins and outs of friendship. Still, those words seem to touch my heart and make me less alone, "Let my heart be according to your heart!" There is an accord I am praying for here, a heart-to-heart with God, that seems to bear upon that of friend with friend. "From the heart," as Beethoven says of his Kyrie, "may it go to the heart!"[28] There is peace in this accord with God, a peace I can taste, that takes away the unpeace of broken friendship. It is indeed the love of God I am remembering, a love exclusive of gods but inclusive of friends, inclusive even of enemies, inclusive all the more of friends who are estranged.

To see God in a friend and to see the friend in God is "to behold the entire world in one ray of the sun." It is to see all in a moment, to enter into a fullness of time. "If I enter into this moment, I will be changed forever," Lin Tan says in Ellen Gilchrist's story "Light Can Be Both Wave and Particle." "If I refuse this moment then I will go about the world as an old man goes, with no hope, no songs to sing, no longing or desire, no miracles of sunlight."[29] If I turn away from spiritual friendship because of the ins and outs of friendship, I will die away from its life and light and love. If I give myself to friendship, though it is "pure suffering" at times as well as "inordinate happiness," I will come to new life and hope, to singing songs and longing desire, to miracles of sunlight. What then of the moments I have refused? Can I recover their life and light and love?

Deserted Places of the Heart

"We imagine divine grace to be finite. For this reason we tremble . . . We tremble before making a choice in life, and after having made it again tremble in fear of having chosen wrong," the General says in his speech at the end of

"Babette's Feast" by Isak Dinesen (Karen Blixen). "But the moment comes when our eyes are opened and we see and realize that grace is infinite . . . See! that which we have chosen is given us, and that which we have refused is, also and at the same time, granted to us. Ay, that which we have rejected is poured upon us abundantly."[30] If this is true, then even the moments I have refused are not lost, and I can recover their life and light and love. In Dinesen's story "Babette's Feast" a young lieutenant comes to a little village in Norway and meets a young woman and they fall in love, but he refuses the moment and goes on to pursue his military career. Years later he comes back as a general and during the feast prepared by Babette he realizes the young woman has always lived in his heart and he discovers that he has always lived in hers. Thus he realizes the possibility he refused all those years ago has nonetheless been given to him.

It is true, living in one another's hearts is not the same as living together. Here is the conversation the two have after the feast:

> He. "I have been with you every day of my life. You know, do you not, that it has been so?"
>
> She. "Yes, I know that it has been so."
>
> He. "And I shall be with you every day that is left to me. Every evening I shall sit down, if not in the flesh, which means nothing, in spirit, which is all, to dine with you, just like tonight. For tonight I have learned, dear sister, that in this world anything is possible . . ."
>
> She. "Yes, it is so, dear brother. In this world anything is possible."[31]

Here is an idea like Kierkegaard's, "God is that all things are possible, and that all things are possible is God."[32] It is linked with that other, "God is spirit." All things are possible if I take into account not only flesh but spirit. For every choice I have made in life there is a road I have taken and there is a road I have not taken. If "grace is infinite," however, and if "all things are possible," I can take also the road I have not taken, "if not in the flesh, which means nothing, in spirit, which is all." The two roads are parallel: I walk one in the flesh but I walk the other in spirit. Or it can happen another way, I have found; the road not taken, for me the way of music, can rejoin the road taken, for me the way of words. So I find myself walking a way of greater wholeness than I thought was possible when I originally chose the way of words and gave up the way of music. When I consider all three, the way of words, the way of music, and the way of spiritual friendship, I begin to believe indeed "all things are possible."

There is a further idea in Dinesen's story, though, and that is Babette's own, who prepares the feast, "Through all the world there goes one long cry from the heart of the artist: Give me leave to do my utmost!"[33] I think of my utmost in words, of my utmost in music, and yet what is your utmost, I ask myself, if not to love "with all your heart, and with all your soul, and with all your might"? And there is that phrase added in the Gospels, to love "with all your mind." Let us see if moving toward such an utmost does not bring all the deserted places of the heart to life and light and love.

Places in the heart become places in memory. There are "places in the heart which do not yet exist," Léon Bloy says, "and into them enters suffering that they may have existence."[34] It is when the "pure suffering" and the "inordinate happiness" of love enters into them that they become places also in memory. When I experience the happiness of having a friend and the suffering of losing my friend, when I experience the gain of a road taken and the loss of a road not taken, the friendship, the road becomes a place in my heart, a place in my memory. Being a place in my heart that exists through the happiness and the suffering of love, it belongs to the wholeness of loving with all my heart. "The only thing in life that is truly whole," the Baal Shem Tov says, "is a broken heart."[35] To love with all my heart thus would be to love with a broken heart, a heart broken by loss. Still, when I realize "grace is infinite" and "all things are possible," when I see the way to recovery of lost friendship and of the road not taken, I am able to love with a broken heart made whole.

Now if I imagine places in memory, I am coming close to the ancient art of memory with its technique of imagining places, imagining the rooms of a house, for instance, or the parts of a theatre, and imaginatively arranging memories there so they can easily be found by walking through from room to room, or from section to section. But if I imagine places in memory to be places also in the heart, I am not as free to organize memory as I would be if my memory theatre were simply a mnemonic device. Instead I have to consider the "reasons of the heart," not just words, for instance, but the way of words, not just music but the way of music, to consider items of memory not just as items but as belonging to a way of life. If "the heart has reasons that reason does not know,"[36] as Pascal says, the reasons belong to a way and come to light as I follow the way.

When I remember the way of words, I am walking in the inhabited places of my heart. I remember learning the names of things:

My grandfather
would take me on a way
that later I would walk alone,
remembering a last
time I had passed a loved
red cedar and a mossyback along
the river running,
—I would stop and point
to see what he would call them,
and whatever he called anything,
that was its name.

I have called this song "Child's Way,"[37] but the way it describes, I realize, has become my way also in later life, as I walk alone, naming "the reasons of the heart." That is what I have been doing in writing, I can see, naming "the reasons of the heart," and it has come out of walking alone, of learning to be willing to walk alone and yet to hope always for companionship. In between my child's way and my way in later life there has come my way of reading and coming to a peaceful vision of coming from God and returning to God. It is this peaceful vision that sustains me, I think, as I look into "the reasons of the heart."

When I remember the way of music, I am walking in deserted places of my heart, or in places that have been deserted until the last few years. I had a dream some years ago in which I heard the words of a command, "Explore the realm of music!" At the time I took it to be metaphorical, a command to explore the realm of feeling. Now, though, I am inclined rather to follow the command into the realm of music itself, a realm where thought and feeling meet, a realm where I discover "reasons of the heart," where "heart" is not just a seat of feeling but "a center of stillness surrounded by silence," as in Dag Hammarskjöld's words introducing the Meditation Room at the United Nations, "We all have within us a center of stillness surrounded by silence."[38] It is out of this silence and stillness, I find, that music arises. I have to be at peace to compose music; I have to be in my own center of stillness; I have to be surrounded by silence.

Deserted places of the heart are like the divine desert of which Meister Eckhart speaks, "where never was seen difference, neither Father, Son, nor Holy Spirit, where there is no one at home, yet where the spark of the soul is more at peace than in itself."[39] These deserted places are filled only with the divine presence, with the silence surrounding our center of stillness. When I begin to live in these deserted places, feeling the peace I find there, then difference begins to exist in them, I and thou, and I begin to be at home in them and they are no longer deserted but inhabited. "I in them, and thou in me,"[40] the formula of indwelling, begins to come true. In the Gospel of John it means Christ in us and God in Christ, and it can mean that here too, an inner light shining in the soul, but it can also mean I am in the deserted places of my heart and my thou is in me, the eternal thou who is my God and also the human thou who is my friend.

To say the desert of the heart is "where the spark of the soul is more at peace than in itself" is to say I find there a sense of wholeness, of being able to love with all my heart. I know Meister Eckhart is speaking of the desert of the divine essence, "the still desert of the Godhead," but I am thinking of the human experience of the All that is the divine essence, "the soul is somehow all things" and "the soul is capable of God." I come to the All by living my unlived life, by inhabiting the deserted parts of my soul, by spending time with music, for instance, and living on the other side of my brain, by spending time with a friend and sharing what is to me the mysterious life of another person. So it is that I am more whole and more at peace in the larger world of words and music than in the world only of words, in the larger world of I and thou than in the world only of myself. I go out into the larger world, nevertheless, as into a still desert.

As I think of music and how my music may be more important to me than to others, as I think of friendship and how our friendship may be more important to me than to my friends, I seem to be walking in a still desert of aloneness. When Meister Eckhart speaks of the divine essence, he may be thinking not so much of beings and of all beings in one as of existence and the wonder of existence, not *how* things are but *that* they are. "Existence is God,"[41] he says (*Esse est Deus*), as if to say the wonder of existence is holy, is divine. It is a wonder I feel when I camp in a desert place where the air is clear and look up into the night sky and see the many stars you can see only in a desert. It is just existence and its wonder, it seems, that is "the still desert of the Godhead." It is a wonder that pervades also my loneliness as I walk in the deserted places of my heart, making music and making friends. Is it enough to make music? Is it enough to make friends? The wonder of existence gives me joy and peace, when I lean back into it, when I am willing to walk alone. Yet my hope is in communion, in words and music and friendship.

Hope and willingness meet in the inner light that is life and light and love. I think of George Herbert's poem "The Call," set to music by Vaughan Williams in his song cycle "Five Mystical Songs."[42] I have been reciting it to myself over and over as I think of the lonely ins and outs of communion in words and music and friendship. I think especially of the last stanza:

> Come my joy, my love, my heart,
> such a joy as none can move,
> such a love as none can part,
> such a heart as joys in love.

A joy that "none can move" is such a joy as you feel in the wonder of existence when you are willing to walk alone. A love that "none can part" is a love where "if you should lose each other . . . do not be afraid, but go on and on." A heart that "joys in love" is a heart for which "all the enjoyment of love is in the love itself." Such a joy, such a love, such a heart is realized when you are willing to walk alone and hope nonetheless for communion with others. Faith is the combination of willingness and hope, and with faith there is a presence of inner light, "that Christ may dwell in your hearts by faith."[43]

Now then if I try to design a memory theatre, after the fashion of the Renaissance, I have three realms of communion to consider, words and music and friendship, but at the heart of all there is aloneness, the communion of "alone with the Alone." Design itself is a realm, but perhaps I can include it simply in the design of the theatre, letting memory take many shapes, as Le Corbusier encoded many shapes into that of his Chapel at Ronchamp. I think of the many specific places that have been shaping for my memory, the Ayasofya in Istanbul, the Church of the Poor Devil on the Amazon, the Rothko Chapel in Houston, the Meditation Room at the United Nations, each one of them not only a memory but also a place of recollection from which I can survey memory. Perhaps I should call what I am imagining here "a memory chapel" rather than "a memory theatre." Letting it take many shapes, I want to suggest a continuum and a memory in which I find things I have not consciously placed there. And placing the communion of "alone with the Alone" at the center, I want to suggest the unity in what William James called "the varieties of religious experience." And seeing aloneness itself as communion, I want to speak to "the transcendence of longing."

"Alone with the Alone" (*solus cum solo*), a phrase I first encountered in Newman's autobiography, goes back to the concluding words of Plotinus in the *Enneads*, "a flight of the alone to the Alone" (*fuge monou pros monon*).[44] There is a detachment, though not a rejection of life, in the willingness to walk alone and to rejoice in the wonder of existence. To be alone with the Alone is a happy aloneness, a communion with the Alone. It is a "flight," to be sure, a flight from unhappy aloneness, a flight from unhappy and destructive relationships with others, but as a communion with God it is at the center of communion with others through words and music and friendship. Say I begin to realize a friendship is not as spiritual as I thought, that I have expectations that leave me and my friend unfree. By letting go of my expectations I come back to a happy aloneness, a communion with the Alone, that allows me to relate to my friend out of fullness rather than emptiness.

I have come across the floor plan of a strange little chapel in the Pyrenees that seems to have the configuration I am imagining here for memory. It is thought to have been a chapel of the Templars.[45] The floor plan is a triangle intersecting three circles at their centers, and the three circles themselves intersect at the center of the triangle. If I take this as the floor plan of my memory theatre or my memory chapel, the three circles are words and music and friendship, and the central point of intersection is the communion of "alone with the Alone." I can easily imagine the triangular shape changing into the pie shape of the Meditation Room at the United Nations and the central point becoming the block of stone there with the ray of light falling upon it. And I can imagine it changing also into the rectangular shape of the Church of the Poor Devil and the octagonal shape of the Rothko Chapel and the circular shape of the Ayasofya, where the center becomes hollow but where "Light flows down,"[46] as Le Corbusier says of his Chapel at Ronchamp. It is the light flowing down, the inner light, that is the unifying element in all the shape changing of memory.

What then is the significance of the light? What do I see "in one ray of the sun"? I think of the ending of Flaubert's *Temptation of Saint Anthony* where after all his temptations Saint Anthony sees the face of Christ shining in the rising sun.[47] I am thinking of how the Quakers call the inner light not only Light Within but also Christ Within. I am thinking of how Christ is the life of the soul in the Gospel of John. *The inner light is the divine presence in the soul, incandescent and iridescent, containing everyone and everything that can be seen in the light.* It is incandescent with the wonder of existence, I want to say, and yet iridescent with the colors of all the things that are.

Say I find myself "at wit's end," thinking about my past and my future. "I need some kindly light," as a friend of mine once said. I find myself waiting on the inner light. What comes first may be closer to willingness than to hope, the willingness to walk alone, and that is the incandescent light of the wonder of existence. Then afterwards there may come something closer to hope, the hope of communion with others, and that is the iridescent light that illumines the particulars of my life with all their many colors. Once I am willing to walk alone, I always seem to find companionship. It is the thing that seems to happen at each great turning point in Tolkien's trilogy. Frodo, the main character, has to come first to a willingness to walk alone—"that rare thing," as Helen Luke comments, "the man who is willing to walk alone"[48]—and then, as soon as he comes to willingness, he finds companions or a companion after all. First he finds Sam and Merry and Pippin, then at the second turning point he finds the whole "fellowship of the Ring," nine companions including himself, and then at the last turning point he finds only his faithful Sam.

If I try to express willingness and hope in sayings as well as in stories, I get into the language of abandon (*l'abandon*), like Jean-Pierre de Caussade writing of "abandonment to divine providence."[49] All the sayings of Caussade ring true, about doing our part and leaving the rest to God, about embracing the present moment, about surrendering to the will of God, about accepting everything with joy, about all being well. Yet there is a distinction I feel I must make here, between the situations of life and the inner light in which we see them. It is the inner light, I want to say, that is the providential guidance of God. It is essential therefore not to surrender or to submit my will to any situation or to any human will but to the inner light alone. If I am willing to walk alone in that light, I become free to hope for my heart's desire.

Now if I pass from words to music, if I sing of willingness and hope, I become a kind of troubadour singing of heart's desire. I feel a need of spiritual change, though, as I stand in the inner light, a need to pass from living in my imagination like a troubadour to loving with all my mind and heart and soul like a saint. I think I can hear the willingness and the hope in plainsong. Maybe that is why plainsong always seems to convey peace of mind and heart and soul. A willingness without hope would be despairing, and a hope without willingness would be strident, but I think I can hear the heart's desire in that peace. If I compose out of that willingness and hope, if I compose out of that peace, I may let myself be influenced by the free rhythm of plainsong, by the modal harmony, by the tendency toward unaccompanied voice. All the same, exploring the realm of music, listening to Mozart for instance, I find that peace of mind is somehow compatible with "the four perturbations of the mind" that also can be expressed in music, desire and gladness and fear and sadness.

It is when I pass from the realm of music into that of friendship that I learn just how peace of mind relates to perturbations of the mind. If I relate to another person out of willingness and hope, a willingness to walk alone and a hope of communion, I am trying to live in peace while remaining vulnerable to perturbation. Yet it is hard to walk alone in the wonder of existence when you are troubled by the ins and outs of a friendship. You are tempted to choose between a happy aloneness and an unhappy love. If I do live in willingness and hope, it seems, I am living in faith, I am living in the inner light. My hope changes, nevertheless, as I continue to live in willingness to walk alone. It changes from setting my heart on someone or something to opening my heart to the mystery of communion, to the mystery of "alone with the Alone" at the heart of "I and thou."

As my hope changes, I come to be more at peace. I begin to see friendship in the "kindly Light" rather than in the

harsh light of expectations that come of living in my imagination, and I begin to let be and be open to the mystery in
friendship. I see how real my willingness to walk alone has
to be to sustain me in peace of mind, how I have to live a
contemplative life of walking with God to sustain a spiritual friendship with another human being. I think of G. K.
Chesterton's lives of saints, of a passage in his life of Saint
Francis of Assisi on being in love with God and of a chapter
in his life of Saint Thomas Aquinas on "The Real Life of
Saint Thomas."[50] I have to be in love with God, I can see, I
have to have a "real life" of walking with God, if I am to be
at peace in a spiritual friendship. In fact, a "real life" with
God, a contemplative life of walking in the wonder of existence, is the communion of "alone with the Alone" that has
to be at the center of my memory theatre where the three
circles of words and music and friendship intersect. If the
center holds, the way of words and music and friendship
opens up before me.

It is a way of "letting be and openness to the mystery." It
is like "abandonment to divine providence." If I keep in
mind, however, the distinction I have made between simple
acceptance of the situations of life and acceptance rather of
the inner light in which we see the situations, I can take "the
mystery" here as something that "shows itself and at the
same time withdraws"[51] in words and in music and in friendship. It shows itself, I want to say, in the inner light; at the
same time it withdraws into the words, into the music, into
the friendship. What is the mystery? Its showing is communion; its withdrawal is aloneness. Its showing and withdrawing is the heartbeat of my life, alone and unalone. It is
the mystery of time.

Of Time
and the Ecstasy of Being Ever

. . . ready to be anything, in the ecstasy of being ever.

—Sir Thomas Browne

Time runs still, time runs deep for me, when I walk alone in the wonder of existence. I want to see my life as a journey in time and God as my companion on the way. "I want to understand time because I want to get close to the Old One," Einstein says in the novel *Einstein's Dreams*.[1] "But there are problems," as Besso points out to Einstein in the novel. "For one, perhaps the Old One is not interested in getting close to his creations, intelligent or not. For another, it is not obvious that knowledge is closeness. For yet another, this time project could be too big for a twenty-six-year-old."

Time comes to light for you when your life opens up before you all the way to death, Heidegger says in *Being and Time*. That began to happen for me around the age of thirty. I began to realize my youth was passing, and I began to see death as the horizon of my life. When you realize you are going to die someday, when you know it in your heart, I mean, and not just in your mind, you come to be conscious of living in time, conscious in a way you never were before. Is such consciousness an understanding of time? Does it

bring you closer to the Old One? It is not the kind of understanding Einstein was looking for, relating time to space and
matter. It is rather a kind relating time to life and death. If
Einstein's understanding of the relativity of time brings us
closer to understanding how "one day is with the Lord as a
thousand years, and a thousand years as one day,"[2] Heidegger's understanding of living toward death seems to take us
further away. Still, if I drop the assumption that death is the
opposite of life and see death rather as an event of life like
birth, then the horizon of my life recedes before me as I approach it, like the horizon of my vision, and living toward
death gives way to living toward life, and I become "ready to
be anything, in the ecstasy of being ever."

"Am I my time?"[3] the question with which Heidegger
ends his early work *The Concept of Time*, calls for a "Yes" from
his point of view. If I say "No" instead, I am making a distinction between the time of my life and the eternal in me.
Walking with God in time, I am walking with the eternal in
time, and that brings out the eternal in me, the person I am,
in contrast with the time of my life. It brings out my heart's
longing, as in Kierkegaard's prayer,

> . . . longing is Thy gift.
> But when longing lays hold of us,
> oh, that we might lay hold of the longing![4]

I feel my heart's longing and it "lays hold" of me, but to walk
with God is to "lay hold of the longing." The eternal relates
to us "when longing lays hold of us," but we relate to the
eternal when we "lay hold of the longing." It is in our heart's
longing that time is relative, that "one day is with the Lord
as a thousand years, and a thousand years as one day."

As I get older and closer to my own death, I can be
tempted ever more to despair of love and to desperation

of longing. But if I can live with an ever receding horizon, believing in eternal life, rather than an ever approaching horizon, imagining my end in death, I can come to "living in love-longing," as Juliana of Norwich calls it, living in love rather than in the despair of love, living in love-longing rather than in the desperation of longing. Let us see what words, what music, what friendship goes into "living in love-longing."[5]

Time and Longing

I know I am living in time when I am feeling the fear of what may happen to me and the regret of what has happened. It is then that my life opens up before me all the way to death. When I am feeling the longing of my heart's desire, on the other hand, I become aware of the horizon of my life receding before me as I approach it. That is "the transcendence of longing," always carrying me beyond any given horizon to a new one. Say I am fearing the loss of the esteem or the loss of the reputation I have enjoyed. What I am fearing really is that the horizon of my life will change. There is something in me, nevertheless, that reaches beyond the horizon anyway, carrying me forward so the horizon does indeed change, and that is the longing of my heart. So it is that love and longing or "love-longing" can cast out fear. I think of the moment at the beginning of Tolkien's trilogy when it is said of Frodo "a great desire flamed up in his heart," a desire to follow in his turn on the adventure, and "It was so strong that it overcame his fear."[6]

It is at the end of *Urne Buriall*, after describing the many ways people want to be buried and have monuments to their memory, that Sir Thomas Browne speaks of faith in eternal life and of being "ready to be anything, in the ecstasy of being ever."[7] Being "ready to be anything" is being heart-free in these matters of burial and remembrance. My fears of losing esteem and of losing reputation, I can see, are much like these fears of being forgotten or of not being honored or even of being dishonored in death. My heart's longing, on the other hand, always leading me on beyond the present horizon of my life, leading me out of my self and out of my fears of losing my self, is "the ecstasy of being ever." Faith in eternal life, it seems, means giving myself over to my heart's longing and its transcendence, letting love have the ascendancy in my life.

Am I ready to be anything, in the ecstasy of being ever? That is the question of living in the transcendence of longing, of living in the faith of eternal life, asking me to pass from a *No*, coming of fear of what I may lose, to a *Yes*, coming of hope of what I may gain on a road going ever on and on. "Eternal life belongs to those who live in the present," as Wittgenstein says, to those who "cast aside regret and fear," as Tolkien says, and "do the deed at hand."[8] But that takes a far-sighted vision, where life opens up before you to the horizon, and the horizon moves as you approach it. If I have no horizon, if I have no hope, I live in quiet desperation, I live in "a horizonless grind." If my horizon is fixed, on the other hand, if my hope is fixed, and my heart is set upon someone or something, I am unable to cast aside regret and fear. If my horizon moves before me, however, if my hope opens before me, if I live really in a moving standpoint, I live in a changing present, I live in a presence in the present, as if I were being led, as if I were walking with God.

"I am" and "I will die," the two great certainties of my life, are transfigured by the sense of presence, of being led, of walking with God. I feel at home, living in the truth, when I say "I am" and "I will die." Can "the practice of the presence of God," the practice of living in the presence, of letting myself be led by the "kindly Light," of walking with God, bring me to a point where I can say, feeling at home and living in the truth, "I am ready to be anything, in the ecstasy of being ever"?

In the Gospel of John "I am" and "I will die" are themselves "the words of eternal life,"[9] spoken as they are in a story of coming from God and returning to God. There is a peaceful vision in that story, it seems to me as I read and reread the Gospel of John, also as I read and reread the *Confessions* of Saint Augustine where it becomes a personal story of wandering away from God and returning to God with tears, also as I read and reread the *Summa*s of Saint Thomas Aquinas where it becomes a universal story of everyone coming from God and returning to God by way of Christ. I can feel the peace when I see myself in the story, and I can feel the unpeace when I stand outside it. To reject the story, Tolkien says, "leads either to sadness or to wrath."[10] When I am feeling sadness or wrath about my own life, it seems I am standing outside the story, and when I am feeling peace, it seems I am standing inside, and when I say "I am" and "I will die" from inside, speaking out of the peace, it seems I too am speaking "the words of eternal life."

It is remarkable, as I think about it, that I can be inside the story at times and at other times outside. It depends on remembering, on reading and remembering, on being in touch with my heart's longing. It is when I have lost touch that I feel the sadness. I think of the Leopardi Fragments set to music by Peter Maxwell Davies:

> Ah! you have passed,
> eternal sigh of mine,
> have passed, and now

>   companion of my every
>   vague imagining,
>   of all my tender sensibilities,
>   of all the movements,
>   sad and dear of heart,
>   is bitter memory.[11]

Here is a description of the sadness and the bitterness, if not of the wrath, that comes of standing outside the story, of losing touch with the heart's longing, "Ah! you have passed, eternal sigh of mine (*eterno sospiro mio*), have passed." My eternal longing has passed, has left me, or I have left my longing, or I have lost touch with my longing, and all that is left is "vague imagining" and "tender sensibilities" and "movements, sad and dear of heart," not a remembering that brings back longing but a "bitter memory."

An eternal longing has inscribed in it the story of coming from God and returning to God. How to tell this story now? Leopardi sees an image of infinity in a steep landscape with peasants descending and disappearing from view, an image of coming and going. He sees it, though, without hope, and it is then he feels eternal longing has deserted him. Looking for such an image, I think of Lawrence of Arabia meeting an old man in the desert who said "The love is from God and of God and towards God."[12] Here the story has become a saying, the moral of a story. If I were to tell the story of which this is the moral, I would not be telling the Platonic story of love, ascending from passion for the individual to ecstasy in contemplation of the ideal, or the Freudian story, finding passion for the individual hidden in ecstasy over the ideal. Instead, I would be finding "the transcendence of longing" and "the ecstasy of being ever" in passion for the individual. The story I tell can be simply the one Lawrence tells of meeting the old man ("all real living is meeting"). Lawrence himself embodies passion for the individual, and the old man embodies the ecstasy of divine love, and the meeting leads Lawrence to insight into love. The story then is one of coming to know the love we do not know.

When a deep loneliness is on me and a sense of loss, I am very near to knowing the love I do not know, very near to remembering the love I have forgotten. It may be reading, as I have found, it may be actually meeting someone, as Lawrence has told, that leads me to know or to remember. And learning here is remembering, not "bitter memory" but bringing to mind what has been hidden in my heart, a re-membering that is a companion to all my imagining and my sensing and all the movements of my heart, that goes with me and guides me, as if it were already my good fortune, as I keep up my heart's expectancy and go to meet whatever is in store for me. To be in the story of coming to know love is to remember I am in the larger story of coming from God and returning to God.

Time is "a changing image of eternity"[13] in the story of coming from God and returning to God, the coming and going of life seen "under the aspect of eternity." I experience the coming and the going, but I also experience the peace of this peaceful vision of coming from God and going to God. Time is the flow of the river, *time is the flow of longing*, the coming and going of all I love, seen in a peaceful vision, seen under the aspect of peace of mind. I was afraid at one time that this peaceful vision was simply my withdrawal into my mind, leaving behind "the perturbations of the mind," leav-ing behind my desire and my gladness, my fear and my sadness. But now it seems to me a peace of mind and heart

and soul, a peaceful eye of the hurricane of desire and gladness and fear and sadness, something upon which all the
perturbations of my mind converge. My heart's longing is
"from God and of God and towards God," I can see in this
peaceful vision, and it is out of my heart's longing that my
desire arises and my gladness and my fear and my sadness.
The darkness of this maelstrom is the darkness of my longing as it goes from one thing to another, from one person to
another, always seeking Someone or Something.

I begin to see now the foolishness of my seeking, always
setting my heart upon someone or something beyond my
reach, maybe sensing in that the transcendence of Someone
or Something I am really seeking. I am like Don Quixote
coming back from his first sally to say "I know who I am,"
from his second to say "I am enchanted,"[14] and from his last
to let go of his illusions and return to his true origin, as if he
too were in a story of coming from God and returning to
God. Seeing myself in the image of Don Quixote, I can say
"I know who I am," I can say "I am enchanted," and yet I can
let go of my illusions and return to my true origin.

"I know who I am," Don Quixote's protest on coming
back from his first sally, sounds very like the Gospel of
John, "I know whence I have come and whither I am
going."[15] My illusions too in setting my heart on someone
or something beyond my reach are very like the truth of my
life in giving my heart to Someone or Something capable
of bringing my restless heart to rest. There is a difference,
though, and it is one of rest in restlessness. When I set my
heart on someone or something beyond my reach, I experience restlessness, I experience time in all the ups and downs
of expectancy and disappointment. When I give my heart to
Someone or Something capable of bringing my heart to rest,

I experience a peace of heart, I experience eternity. Or rather, I experience rest in restlessness, eternity in time, I experience time as "a changing image of eternity." Say I am feeling tantalized, teased, tormented by someone or something I have set my heart on, showing like mystery and at the same time withdrawing. All I can do is give myself to what truly is mystery and rest in its showing and withdrawing.

"I am enchanted" I can say like Don Quixote coming back from his second sally. I have been under a spell, tantalized, teased, tormented by the mystery I have found in whoever or whatever I have set my heart on, but now I have begun to see there is a way to break the spell, and that is "letting be" (*Gelassenheit*) or really "letting be and openness to the mystery," not turning away but turning toward the mystery, letting be and becoming heart-free. As I come to be heart-free in my relationship to that someone or something, I come to be at peace and the mystery I have found there begins to seem transcendent, to lie beyond the person, beyond the thing I took to be my heart's desire. Still, there is heart in heart-free and I do not lose heart.

Losing heart is the thing I most fear in giving up my illusions, in letting be and becoming heart-free. If there is heart, though, in heart-free, then returning to my true origin like Don Quixote at the end is not the sad thing it is taken to be. "I was mad, but I am sane now,"[16] he says. He is at peace now in his awareness of his mortality as he never was in his madness, crazed as he was by reading the romances of chivalry. Although his madness came of reading stories, there is a story, as I have been finding, that brings peace of mind, and that is the story of coming from God and returning to God. The difference seems to lie in the identity you have in this story, that of a little creature in a big world made by God, "I am" coming from God and "I will die" returning to God, a great relief from the inflation and the wounded pride you suffer trying to live in a romance. "I was Don Quixote de la Mancha," Don Quixote says at the end, "but today I am Alonso Quixano called the Good." There is still a dignity in who he is, "called the Good," but the inflation is gone of being "Don Quixote de la Mancha." Humility is the way of peace, and "humility is endless," is everlasting life.

It is from inside the endlessness of humility, from inside the story of coming from God and returning to God, that the adventures of Don Quixote appear comic. Or if I make a distinction beween wit and humor, it is from inside the endlessness of humility that his adventures appear humorous. From inside romance Don Quixote can seem a tragic figure. (Speaking out of "the tragic sense of life" Unamuno calls him "Our Lord Don Quixote".)[17] It is in a passage criticizing the wisdom of old age that T. S. Eliot says "The only wisdom we can hope to acquire is the wisdom of humility: humility is endless,"[18] and then he goes on to speak of mortality, of everything passing away. Don Quixote's wisdom at the end is just this, a wisdom in the face of death, of all things passing away, not a wisdom that is a sum total of his life, a sum of all his adventures. It is the wisdom of humility, but then the wisdom of the end is itself endless, "humility is endless." Death here is an event of life like birth, not the opposite of life (as in "the tragic sense of life"), and so the wisdom of death is not a summing up but an opening onto infinity.

I think of Saint Augustine on his deathbed, reciting the Seven Penitential Psalms, still repenting as he had already done years before in his *Confessions*. Of course repenting is itself a summing and a letting go, a remembering that is a letting go. Who I am in such a remembering is not my life but the one who lives my life. There is a distinction, I mean, between me and my life, between the person and the life lived, that comes to light in remembering and letting go. It is a distinction that opens onto infinity, as the person I am can live on beyond the life I have lived. Just as my life is linked with time, my person is linked with eternity, is the eternal in me. If time is the flow of longing, the eternal in me is the unfulfilled capacity that is expressed in the longing, the soul "capable of God," the heart "restless until it rests in you." Repentance is a remembering that is a letting go of everyone and everything other than the One in whom the heart finds repose. There can be a concern for esteem even in repentance, it is true. "May my sincere repentance restore your former esteem for me,"[19] Don Quixote says on his deathbed. To let go even of esteem is to be "ready to be anything, in the ecstasy of being ever."

My own remembering and letting go has a way to go before I will be "ready to be anything," I can see now, but I can feel something of "the ecstasy of being ever" in my hope of eternal life and eternal vision. I can feel "our heart is restless until it rests in you," I can feel the restlessness, that is, and in moments of peace I can feel the rest, and I can feel the hope arising out of these moments of rest in restlessness. It is a hope of eternal life and light and love, a hope coming out of the inner light and peace I can feel when I am living in the peaceful eye of my storm of "perturbations of the mind." I think of loving "with all your mind" and of saints longing for the eternal vision of God and of my own feeling for the peaceful vision of coming from God and returning to God.

My reading and coming to serenity is not unlike Don Quixote reading and coming to adventure. Reading is "a communication in the midst of solitude,"[20] Proust says in his essay *On Reading*. When I read the Gospel of John, I am communing in solitude in a vision of coming from God and returning to God, and when I read the *Confessions* of Saint Augustine, I am communing in solitude in a vision of wandering away from God and returning to God in tears. When I commune not in solitude but in a to-and-fro with persons I know in my life, serenity moves into the background of my experience while "the perturbations of the mind" come into the foreground, desire and gladness, fear and sadness. As a background, nevertheless, serenity shines through the perturbations of the foreground so they no longer seem perturbations but adventures of the heart. Time seems "a changing image of eternity" and the persons who enter my life and the situations that arise in my life seem to belong to my life. The story of coming from God and returning to God becomes my own story.

What is essential about this story, according to Tolkien, is the happy ending, the "eucatastrophe," as he says "This story begins and ends in joy."[21] There is catastrophe in eucatastrophe, though, death as well as birth and rebirth. The joy is not simple gladness but eternity shining through time, serenity shining through the adventures and misadventures of the heart. There are times of eclipse too, when eternity does not shine through and I seem to be lost in time, when serenity does not shine through and I seem to be lost in the adventures and the misadventures of my heart. It is then I find myself waiting on joy, praying "Come my joy, my love, my heart . . . ," waiting really on eternity in time, waiting for time to become translucent. At those times the endlessness of humility seems to be a way back into the sense of joy.

"Humility provides everyone, even the lonely and despairing, with the firmest relation to one's fellow human beings," Kafka says. "Our relation to our fellow human beings is that of prayer, our relation to ourselves, that of striving," he says. "From prayer we draw the strength for striving."[22] Humility is a relationship with other human beings, as he understands it, a relationship of prayer where I recognize the mystery in others, the thing in them I do not know or control, where I stand with them before God. If I am willing to enter into that relationship when I feel "lonely and despairing," I can find hope and strength to keep on striving. The willingness leads me into the hope. If I go from living in my imagination like Don Quixote to differentiating between imagination and reality as he does on his deathbed, I am humbling myself, but I have still to integrate reality and imagination, and that is when I realize "humility is endless" and begin to recover my hope and my joy. Willingness differentiates but hope integrates.

Willingness differentiates by accepting the mystery in human life, the mystery that tantalizes us by showing itself and at the same time withdrawing. Hope integrates by finding the way of possibility, the way of the heart's desire. The theme song in Tolkien's song cycle and in his trilogy sings of the way:

> The Road goes ever on and on
>   Down from the door where it began.
> Now far ahead the Road has gone,
>   And I must follow, if I can,
> Pursuing it with eager feet,
>   Until it joins some larger way
> Where many paths and errands meet.
>   And whither then? I cannot say.[23]

If "humility is endless," then its road "goes ever on and on." The path of humility is the way of the heart's desire.

When Longing Lays Hold of Us

"We say God and the imagination are one . . . ," Wallace Stevens has in a poem called "Final Soliloquy of the Interior Paramour,"[24] speaking from a standpoint integrating reality and imagination. One but not the same. If imagination is our faculty of possibility, then it is our key to understanding "God is that all things are possible, and that all things are possible is God." Still, it does not make all things possible. When I am feeling very alone, I imagine all kinds of things, many of them untrue. I may feel abandoned by my friends, when in fact they still love me. It is rather "when longing lays hold of us," when our heart is kindled and our mind illumined, that "We say God and the imagination are one . . . ," for it is then that the way of possibility opens before us. Say I have been feeling alone and friendless, but say I let my interior soliloquy, my conversation with myself, become a prayer, a conversation with the inner light, like Newman's "Lead, Kindly Light." As soliloquy becomes prayer, my longing lays hold of me and the way of possibility opens before me:

> Lead, kindly Light,
>   amid the encircling gloom—
>   Lead Thou me on!
> The night is dark,
>   and I am far from home—
>   Lead Thou me on!
> Keep Thou my feet;
>   I do not ask to see the distant scene—
>   one step enough for me.[25]

Saying this prayer, or singing this song, I find my relation with myself has gone from one of striving to one of prayer.

I realize the mystery that "shows itself and at the same time withdraws" is in me as well as in others, showing me the way, showing the next step, "one step enough for me," but withdrawing when I want "to see the distant scene."

A conversation with myself, a "soliloquy of the interior paramour," when it becomes prayer, becomes a conversation with God. Not that I become God to myself, but I recognize the presence of something greater than myself. The oneness or union of God and the imagination is the presence of God in our faculty of possibility, kindling the heart and illumining the mind, as the way of possibility opens before us. It is very much otherwise when the heart is in darkness before the kindling and illumining, for then "the imagination of the heart," as it is called in Scripture, can be a destructive force. It was after a brush with death when he was a young man traveling in Sicily that Newman wrote the lines "Lead, kindly Light." In the delirium of his fever he was saying "I shall not die, I shall not die, for I have not sinned against the light, I have not sinned against the light."[26] It is as if he were wandering in the imagination of his heart during his fever and then emerged to write those peaceful lines about the "kindly Light."

I can be lost, I can wander alone in the imagination of my heart, but then my heart can be kindled and my mind illumined, and I can find the way of possibility. Grace is the kindling of the heart and the illumining of the mind, I am thinking; it is being known and loved by God when being known becomes an illumining and being loved a kindling. And the way of possibility is the way on which you become capable of love, able to love "with all your heart, and with all your soul, and with all your might." It is "when longing lays hold of us," when our hearts are kindled and our minds illumined, that we are capable of love. How then to find the way, how come to the kindling and the illumining? Is it by letting our interior soliloquy become prayer?

Our sense of time changes as we pass from soliloquy to prayer and come to a sense of eternity. If Plato's philosophy is "an endless conversation,"[27] it becomes for Saint Augustine an endless conversation with self in his *Soliloquies* and ten years later in his *Confessions* an endless conversation with God. My life is already an endless conversation, a passing over into the lives of others and a coming back into my own life with whatever insight I gain from seeing with the eyes and feeling with the heart of others. But what do I see with my own eyes? What do I feel in my own heart? Those are questions leading into an endless conversation with myself, or *also* with myself, as others are still present to me as I commune with myself. I realize I want to know myself as well as others, and in coming to know myself I realize I want to know God, to know what is greater than myself, and that leads me on into an endless conversation with God, or *also* with God, as I am present to myself and others are present to me as I commune with God.

It is at the high point of soliloquy, when it becomes prayer, that my heart is kindled and my mind illumined. Saint Augustine begins his *Soliloquies* saying "I want to know God and the soul," then halfway through he prays "May I know me, may I know thee," and then towards the end, "Let me return to me, let me return to thee."[28] If I can pray in this way, my prayer can be an expression of my heart's longing. By giving it expression I allow myself to feel my longing. It is true, just saying the words won't do it. There is a direction in the prayer and there is an energy, and the direction can be there without the energy. If I turn in the direction, though, the energy may come, gathering from the four winds of desire where it has been dissipated. It is by turning in that direction, it seems, by prayer rather than by striving, that I come to the energy.

"Thus everything depends on this: that our thinking should become more thoughtful in its season," Heidegger says. "This is achieved when our thinking, instead of implementing a higher degree of exertion, is directed toward a different point of origin."[29] He has in mind thinking back to Being, but what he says seems true of thinking back to God. Thinking back to Being means remembering the wonder of existence, the wonder that all things are. Thinking back to God means remembering the wonder of my own existence, the wonder that I am. When I remember the wonder that I am, the wonder that I exist at all, I become a mystery to myself and my thou becomes a mystery to me, I want to "know me," to "know thee." "Sometimes I miss God," a friend wrote, becoming thoughtful about loneliness. "But you know sometimes, when I think I am farthest from God, I feel at this time closest. The pain of being away from Him and the fear of not being able to find my way back to Him lets me know how much I love Him." The pain and the fear of my loneliness makes me realize my longing for God and my love of God.

But then there are times when my longing seems otherwise, when I long for another human being to love and to know, times when I meet with disappointment too as the other's longing seems always less than mine. "There is no one here who has an understanding for me in full," Kafka writes in his diary. "To have even one who had this understanding, for instance a woman, would be to have support from every side. It would be to have God."[30] Still, if my longing is like

Kafka's, then even here it is a longing to "know me," to "know thee." Only it takes the shape of a longing to have another person know me, to have someone else understand me in full, and thus to find support, to find God. What have I been expecting of others? To realize my longing, I can see, is to let my human relations be human. Yet it seems it is in these relations that I do come to "know me," to "know thee."

"I in them, and thou in me,"[31] the formula in the Gospel of John, comes true for me as my conversation with others deepens and continues in a conversation with myself, "I in them," and a conversation with God, "and thou in me." There is always a circle of friends present in these discourses I have been reading and rereading, the Gospel of John, the *Soliloquies* and the *Confessions* of Augustine. And there is no modern idea of autonomy or self-sufficiency, though these very discourses are the historic sources of the idea of autonomy (Augustine even coined the word "soliloquy," *soliloquium*). I am always stumbling over the barrier of autonomy as I go back and forth between self and others and between self and God. I begin to see how "an endless conversation," if that barrier is not erected, can well become an endless conversation with self and with God. If "I in them, and thou in me," as it stands in the Gospel of John, means Christ present in his disciples as inner life and light and love and therefore as the presence of God, then if I say "I in them, and thou in me," it means I am connected with others by way of the presence of God, that my relation with them, as Kafka says, is a relation of prayer, and comes to its fulfilment in prayer, in an endless conversation with God.

"Even if Kafka did not pray—and this we do not know— he still possessed in the highest degree what Malebranche called 'the natural prayer of the soul': attentiveness," Walter

Benjamin says. "And in this attentiveness he included all living creatures, as saints include them in their prayers."[32] There is direction in attentiveness, and there is energy, and including all the persons who belong to my life in my prayer enables me to bring all my life into my prayer, to be in it myself, and thus to be myself before God, like Saint Augustine in his *Confessions*, recollecting his life before God and bringing to mind all the persons of his life. As I think back to the wonder of existence and to the wonder of my own existence, I see all the persons of my life as *belonging* to my life. That is how I see them in prayer, and that is how I come to know myself and to know God.

Thinking back to the wonder of my own existence, I mean, I can include all the persons of my life in my prayer, and thinking back to the wonder of all existence, like Saint Augustine at the end of his *Confessions*, thinking back not just to his own birth but to the beginning of time, I can include "all living creatures" in my prayer. I can come to know myself then in relation to the persons of my life but also in relation to "all living creatures." I can come in that way upon the eternal in me, upon the mystery that shows itself in me and at the same time withdraws into all else. If I name the mystery "thou," if I pray, that is, I am entering into a personal relationship with God, relating to God as personal rather than impersonal. At the same time I am entering into an "I and thou" with the persons of my life and with "all living creatures," including them in my prayer, relating to a person in the persons and in all living beings. I am entering, that is, into a personal relationship with the mystery showing and withdrawing in all, and my relationship is one of prayer, of waiting on God, waiting in the withdrawing, waiting always on the showing.

"We have plenty of time," Socrates says, speaking out of "an endless conversation," and "we have time enough," Augustine says in his *Soliloquies*, and "we are to do nothing but wait," Heidegger says in his "Conversation on a Country Path."[33] When your life opens up before you all the way to death, it doesn't seem there is plenty of time or time enough or there is nothing to do but wait—on the contrary, it seems you have to make the most of what little time there is. If I say "we have plenty of time" or "we have time enough," I am living in a perspective where time is relative, where "one day is with the Lord as a thousand years, and a thousand years as one day," and if I say "we are to do nothing but wait," I am living in a perspective where time is "the lighting up of the self-concealing,"[34] as in Heidegger's later thinking, where time is the showing of a mystery that withdraws.

Showing and withdrawing, that is the rhythm of the mystery in time. It is the showing that illumines the mind, but it is the withdrawing that kindles the heart with longing. Say I fear being netted like a bird (I dreamt the other night of an eagle flying down and being covered with a close fitting net). I fear a situation confining me to myself in my loneliness. My fear is the other side of a longing,

> O give us wings, for the faithful
> Voyage and the return![35]

as Hölderlin prays in his poem "Patmos." It is a "faithful voyage" and there is a "return," but we need "wings," and as he says "where the danger lies, there likewise lies the salvation." I long for wings to make the faithful voyage into danger and to return with salvation, to pass over into other lives where I find the mystery and to come back again to find the mystery also in myself. The danger is in a loss of self, to lose myself in crossing the boundaries between myself and others, between myself and the mystery, but there too is the salvation, to come into touch with what is greater than myself.

Say I try to pass over into the Gospel of John, as Hölderlin does in "Patmos," to pass over into the flight of the eagle (that symbol of John the evangelist):

> In darkness dwell
> The eagles: fearless the sons
> Of the Alps pass over the abyss
> On delicate bridges.

The flight of the eagle in the Gospel of John is from the high place where he begins, "In the beginning was the Word . . ." and follows the coming of the Word into the world, "The light shines in the darkness," and the return of the Word to God, "and the darkness has not overcome it."[36] I can pass over into this insofar as I can see myself, and all of us, living in this story, being led by the kindly light shining in the darkness, shining not only in the darkness of life but even in that of death.

"In darkness dwell the eagles," Hölderlin says, and that is the darkness in which the light shines, a darkness of unknowing, a night of sense and spirit. If I let myself be led by the kindly light, I can be "fearless," unafraid of the dark, and I can "pass over the abyss" of life and death "on delicate bridges," bridges I can make out in the kindly light. What I fear is a life like Hölderlin's in his later years of madness, "a life curiously bleak, empty and solitary."[37] That is a more profound darkness with fewer glimmers of light. All I can do is follow such light as I have, such light as is given to me, trusting the saying of Jesus in the Gospel of John, "one who follows me will not walk in darkness,"[38] the saying with which *The Imitation of Christ* begins, and at times when my own life seems "curiously bleak, empty and solitary," I have to look for what glimmer of light I can find, and cherish it and follow it, making as much of it as I can.

It is just at such times, when my life seems bleak and empty and solitary, that I can be on the verge of a kindling of the heart and an illumining of the mind. What a spiritual guide "looks for in a soul is what the soul itself is hoping for," Abbé Huvelin says, "that special feeling of emptiness produced by God himself in the soul, the point at which God demands something of it."[39] My bleakness, my emptiness, my solitariness is my experience of unrequited longing. It can turn into a passionate longing when it is kindled with hope, and when it is kindled it is capable of illumining my life and my way ahead. It is then, in the kindling and the illumining, that it seems to be God asking something, even demanding something of me. It is also me asking something, even demanding something of God.

"God requires the heart,"[40] as is said in the Talmud, and the heart requires God. I have thought about this before, but I see it more clearly now. The very thought that God requires my heart kindles my heart. I can feel "a life curiously bleak, empty and solitary" turn into an adventure, into a journey with God in time. Somehow this unconditional demand for my heart is much more exciting for me than an unconditional acceptance of me in my bleakness and emptiness and solitariness. It pulls me right out of such a life and sets me on my adventure with God. The kindly light of God's leading illumines the bleak landscape of my life and with its own warmth takes away the sense of cold and lifelessness. It reveals many signs and forms that were hidden from my eyes when the landscape seemed empty. And though it is an inner light, not an outer light like the sun, it keeps me company and takes away my sense of being solitary. If God requires my heart, I realize my heart requires God; I realize it just seeing how the kindly light changes the aspect of my life.

"I see it! I see it!" a student of mine came in saying one day. "What do you see?" I asked him. "You accept death," he said, "and then you are free," free to live, he meant, free to love. He had been reading the mystics but he had discovered there "an impassioned freedom towards death"[41] such as Heidegger describes in *Being and Time*. I can see the acceptance of death. Still, seeing my life and death in the kindly light of God's leading, I pass from living toward death to living toward eternal life. Am I still free, still free to live, still free to love? I become very aware of God asking something, even demanding something of me, of God requiring my heart, but as I become aware also of myself asking something, even demanding something of God, of my heart requiring God, I realize I am indeed free, I am indeed free to live, I am indeed free to love.

It is true, this freedom is not to do whatever you choose. Rather it is an ability to love, a capability of loving "with all your heart, and with all your soul, and with all your might." To be free, according to this, is to be capable of love; to be unfree is to be incapable of love. "Will it come, or will it not, the day when the joy becomes great, the day when the grief becomes small?" Dag Hammarskjöld asks himself, quoting from a Swedish poet. "It *did* come—the day when the grief became small," he answers himself. "For what had befallen me and seemed so hard to bear became insignificant in the light of the demands which God was now making," he says, speaking of the loneliness that had befallen him and how it became insignificant in the light of God requiring his heart for the work he wanted him to do. "But how difficult it is to feel that this was also, and for that very reason, the day when the joy became great,"[42] he adds, speaking no doubt of the loneliness he still feels even while feeling God is asking something of him. It is the call of God, the requiring of my heart, that makes the grief of loneliness seem small, that makes me capable of giving my heart, but the joy becomes great as I realize my heart requires God.

"Love and do what you will,"[43] Augustine's saying, comes true for me as I realize my heart requires God, not "Accept death and then you are free" so much as "Accept love and then you are free." There is a freedom that comes of accepting death, but it becomes a more determinate freedom in accepting love, for then the orientation of love becomes my life's direction, and what I will is in accord with love. On a day when I have been engrossed in the trivial things of my life, I can get back in touch with the essential by remembering my own death, *memento mori*. I see in the light of death that love is essential, that what matters in all my human relations is to be in love with God. How then do I make love my life's direction? How do I go from living toward death to living toward eternal life?

When We Lay Hold of the Longing

There is a "secret sun, dark with excess of light, or not showing its light save in the enlightenment of others," Chesterton says, that "might well be the exact emblem of that inner and ideal life of the saint."[44] The inner light that shines for faith is that "secret sun, dark with excess of light," the light that shines when the heart's longing that we all have is kindled with hope. It is a "secret sun" because it is an inner not an outer light. It is "dark with excess of light" like a dark star, radiant and yet invisible, "not showing its light save in the enlightenment of others," for it is the light of an "inner and ideal life." We all have an inner life of some kind, but it may not be at all an ideal life. If I live largely in my imagination like Don Quixote, that black sun begins to shine in my life when I embrace my own death, as he does at the end of the story, when I embrace it in the hope of eternal life.

It is through willingness to die and hope to live that we "lay hold of the longing." There is a letting go of everyone and everything in the willingness to die, but there is a reaching out toward life and light and love in the hope to live. Thus the "inner and ideal life of the saint" (Chesterton is thinking of Saint Thomas Aquinas) is pervaded by a longing for eternal vision, can be summed up in a prayer for vision, "Nothing, Lord, but you," can reach a point of vision beyond words, "I can write no more . . ."[45] Vision because that "secret sun" shines in such a way that I perceive things in its light without perceiving the sun disc itself, "dark with excess of light." That black sun is eternal life wearing the mask of death, eternal light wearing the mask of darkness, eternal love wearing the mask of loneliness.

If I take the "vision of God"[46] to be God's vision, however, as Nicholas of Cusa does, then our experience of it is a sense of being known and loved by God. It is a sense of being known before it is a sense of knowing, a sense of being loved before it is a sense of loving. That black sun is a sun whose rays can be felt in being known and loved before its own disc can be seen in knowing and loving. I can see it is willingness and hope that give me access to the sense of being known and being loved, but then my journey in time, my spiritual adventure, takes me from being known to knowing, from being loved to loving. It is willingness to die and hope to live that give me entry into the story of coming from God and returning to God, the story I have been finding in the Gospel of John and the *Confessions* of Augustine. Through being known and loved I have a sense of coming from God; through knowing and loving I have a sense of returning to God. I see then essentially what I have to do to live "that inner and ideal life of the saint." I have to find my way from being known and loved to knowing and loving.

To know and be known, to love and be loved, is ultimately one and the same thing, it seems, to be caught up in our heart's longing. "Prayer and poverty," my spiritual director once said to me: "Christ becomes your whole life, and everything else drops away." If I think of the Christ Within, as the Quakers say, the Light Within, this would mean I have to let go of everyone and everything, as in death, to follow the inner light that is life and love. I find myself following then the trajectory from God to God. I go from realizing I am known and I am loved to realizing I do know and I do love.

"In place of death there was light," Tolstoy says at the end of his story *The Death of Ivan Ilych*. "So that's what it is!" Ivan Ilych exclaims. "What joy!"[47] When I am living toward death, I don't yet realize this. It is only when I go through death, as it were, letting go of everyone and everything, it is only when "everything else drops away," that I "see the light." Still, those words, "prayer and poverty," seem to imply that prayer comes first, before poverty, that "the natural prayer of the soul: attentiveness" comes before the letting go of everyone and everything, before "everything

else drops away." Paying attention to everyone and everything in my life is already a letting be and an openness to
their mystery. It is a letting be that is a turning toward rather
than a turning away. It can become a letting go because letting them be, respecting their own integrity, I release them
from my expectations. It was through my expectations that I
held on to them. I am like Ivan Ilych on his deathbed, trying
to say "Forgive" and instead saying "Forgo."

These deathbed scenes I am invoking from literature, Don
Quixote on his deathbed, Ivan Ilych on his deathbed, are
reenacted for me in the midst of life. I can seem to be living
all the more toward death, and yet there is a difference here
from Heidegger's "being toward death" and his "impassioned
freedom toward death." It is that by going through death,
letting go of everyone and everything, I somehow put death
behind me rather than ahead of me, and I find myself living
toward eternal life. My sense of my self changes as I begin
to taste "the ecstasy of being ever" and to realize I live in
eternal knowledge and love. My sense of "being ever" is a
sense of being known and loved, a sense of being called to
know and love. My life, I can see, is about learning to love.

"One who loves God cannot strive that God should love
one back," Spinoza says, but that is because "the love of God
for human beings and the mind's intellectual love of God is
one and the same."[48] It is like being caught up in a river of
love that comes from God and goes to God. Still, I can realize I am known and loved before I realize I know and love. It
is a matter of realization to know and to love as well as to be
known and to be loved, as if knowing and loving were happening in my life as well as being known and being loved
without my realizing it. Of course it makes a great difference
to realize it. I once came across a definition of "realize" that

surprised and enlightened me, that to "realize" is to "imagine vividly." Living in my imagination like Don Quixote, I at once understand and am wary of such a definition. Here the definition seems to call on me to use all my powers of imagination to enter into knowledge and love:

> Realize (as here compared . . .) implies a very vivid conception or imagination of something that does exist or has existed or may exist, but which is not known through the senses or through experience: the term suggests such vividness that the thing conceived seems actual or true.[49]

"Realize" is here compared with "think," "conceive," "imagine," "fancy," "envisage," and "envision." To think of love, to conceive of love, to imagine love, to fancy love, to envisage love, to envision love is less than to realize love. Novalis called Spinoza "a man inebriated with God."[50] To realize the love of God, to enter imaginatively into the love of God, is to become caught up in the love of God. "God becomes your whole life," we can say, "and everything else drops away." Prayer here is contemplation of God, like Spinoza's, seeing God in everyone and everything, letting God fill your thoughts and feelings. Poverty is the spiritual freedom that Spinoza prized, not freedom from emotions so much as freedom from emotional attachments.

If I say instead "Christ becomes your whole life, and everything else drops away," I am speaking of entering imaginatively into the story of coming from God and returning to God. Prayer here, "the natural prayer of the soul: attentiveness," becomes attentiveness to the persons entering my life, to the situations arising in my life, taking them as belonging to my life, as coming from God, and thus taking my life and myself as coming from God. If I see the persons and situations of my life as coming from God, I see myself as being led, as being called to enter into an "I and thou" with the persons, into an "I and it" with the situations, discerning my relationship with them in the inner light. And in seeing myself as being led, being guided step by step, I am seeing myself as being known and being loved. My being known takes the form of an illumining of my mind as I see how persons and situations belong to my life. And my being loved takes the form of a kindling of my heart as the way opens up before me.

"But all things excellent are as difficult as they are rare,"[51] Spinoza concludes after speaking of spiritual freedom. That is true also of the sense of being known and loved by God— it is very spiritual, not as tangible as being known and loved by another human being. To be caught up in divine love is indeed "excellent" and "difficult" and "rare," and when it is intense it is perhaps more a sense of knowing God and loving God, like Spinoza's, than a sense of being known and being loved. But if I go with the sense of being known and loved, however subtle, if I go with the sense of being led, I can come to that vivid sense of knowing and loving. As it is, my sense of being known and loved can be overshadowed by the intensity of my loneliness. In those lonely moments I believe in the love without feeling the love, and I realize it is by believing in love that I come to feel love.

"Even love must pass through loneliness,"[52] Wendell Berry begins his poem "Setting Out." Entering the story of coming from God and returning to God, I enter a story where there is a far point from God, farthest from the beginning and from the end in God, like the far point in the orbit of a planet or a comet around the sun, the aphelion. I have to go away from God before I can come back to God, and so I have to feel the loneliness of distance before I can return to intimacy. Or that is the way I try to make sense of the loneliness I feel. There is a longing in the loneliness, the longing to be unalone, and that is my heart's longing, and that is what becomes the love of God when my longing is filled with the hope of fulfilment. Meanwhile I do feel the loneliness and the longing in the loneliness, and that loneliness and longing has to be love to me, "love-longing" maybe, as Juliana called it, and the matrix out of which my love can be kindled and rekindled.

"Night cometh,"[53] that ominous sentence in the Gospel of John, seems to speak of this far point from God, the point farthest out in coming from God and returning to God. It is "the dark night of the soul" of which the mystics speak, "the night of sense" and "the night of spirit." For me it is this loneliness I feel. All the same, it is the turning point where coming from God goes over into returning to God. There are two elements in loneliness: the sense of being alone and the longing to be unalone. They exist in a kind of unsteady balance with each other. But as the longing begins to prevail over the aloneness, as it becomes consciously a longing for union or reunion, I find myself on the road of return, on "the road of the union of love with God."[54]

"God and my heart are weeping together,"[55] as is said in one of Grimm's fairy tales. I begin to realize, that is, that my loneliness is God's love in me, that my longing is God's longing in me. When Spinoza says "the love of God for human beings and the mind's intellectual love of God are one and the same," he is speaking of the longing as it exists in the mind, and how our longing to know and God's longing to be known to us are one. When I say "God and my heart are weeping together," I am speaking of the longing as it exists in the heart, and how our longing for union or reunion and God's are one. But to realize God's love and ours are one, to realize "God and my heart are weeping together," is to realize a oneness with God that is already a union or reunion. The fairy tale I am quoting here is one that was discovered in recent years in a letter Grimm wrote to a little girl in 1816 and was kept by her family ever since. It is indeed a story of union or reunion, the story of a little girl who was sent by her mother into a forest to escape a war that was about to engulf their home and how the little girl meets there her guiding and guarding spirit.

It is also, as Grimm says in his letter to the little girl, a story in which "one human heart goes out to another, undeterred by what lies between," his own heart going out to her whom he has never met, undeterred by their distance. When I am feeling my own loneliness, my heart too goes out to another human heart, "undeterred by what lies between," though there is something Quixotic about being undeterred. At the same time, realizing "God and my heart are weeping together" in my loneliness, I begin to realize I am not alone and my heart going out to another human heart is God in me going out to another heart. "Thus does my heart go out to you," Grimm says, "and though my eyes have not seen you yet, it loves you and thinks it is sitting beside you."

Here I am indeed using the powers of my imagination to enter into the love of God, and yet what I am doing is "realizing" the love insofar as the love is something real. When the little girl in the story says "God and my heart are weeping together," she is speaking of the rain falling as her heart weeps. She has been feeling heavy of heart with dread and has prayed for help to go on into the forest. As her heart begins then to feel lighter, and rain begins to fall, she says

God and her heart are weeping together. So it is for me, when I am feeling heavyhearted with loneliness and let the longing in my loneliness become prayer, it is then I feel God and my heart are weeping together. Instead of being simply alone I realize I am "alone with the Alone," and instead of simply longing I realize my longing is also God's longing. The essential thing then, as in the story, is to let the longing in my loneliness become prayer. "Oh, dear God, help your child to go on," the little girl prays in the story. "Oh, dear God, help your child to go on," I pray too, and immediately I realize I am not walking alone but am walking with God on a journey in time.

If I say then "God and my heart are weeping together," as the little girl does in the story, I am entering imaginatively into the love of God, "realizing" the love of God, seeing with God's eyes, as it were, and feeling with God's heart. I am aware, nevertheless, that my vision is an imaginative one, and in all my "realizing" I am aware of my unknowing. It is an unknowing, I am hoping, such as in "the cloud of unknowing, in the which a soul is oned with God."[56] Trying to enter imaginatively into the love of God, trying to "realize" love while being aware that to "realize" is to "imagine vividly," I am conscious of imagining, I am conscious thus of unknowing. Insofar as I really do become caught up in the love of God, though, "a soul is oned with God."

I am "ready to be anything, in the ecstasy of being ever," therefore, *when I let the longing in my loneliness become prayer and I begin to be caught up in the love of God*. Just as "one human heart goes out to another, undeterred by what lies between," so in prayer a human heart goes out to God's heart, undeterred by the lonely feeling of distance ("Oh, dear God, help your child to go on"), and "realizing" the love of God, entering imaginatively into the love, that is, becomes caught up in the love of God ("God and my heart are weeping together"). And to be caught up in the love of God is to be caught up "in the ecstasy of being ever," as God becomes your whole life, and to be "ready to be anything," as everything else drops away. All the same, "one human heart goes out to another" in that loneliness, "undeterred by what lies between" one human being and another. "Thus does my heart go out to you," the storyteller says, "and though my eyes have not seen you yet, it loves you and thinks it is sitting beside you." So the "I and thou" with God becomes also an "I and thou" of one human being with another.

It is as if storytelling between one human being and another were like prayer between a human being and God. If I see us as living in a story and ask "What story are we in?" as I often do ask myself, I take things happening as having a meaning, like the incidents in a story, and I take some things as signs of things past or of things to come, and in choosing my way I find myself waiting for my heart to speak and waiting also for the way to open up before me. All of this, I think, is "the natural prayer of the soul: attentiveness," paying attention to things happening, to signs, to the heart speaking, to the way opening. It is a way of relating to God but also a way of relating to other persons. It is attentiveness to God and to human beings and really to "all living creatures."

Now if I answer my question about what story we are in with the story of coming from God and returning to God, as I have been doing here, I am saying "time's arrow" becomes love's direction, time's direction from past to future becomes love's direction from God to God. I am implying thus a relativity of time as in Grimm's story where the little girl goes into the forest for what to her are three days but what proves to be thirty years when she comes back to find her mother. It is as if to say "one day is with the love of God as a thousand years, and a thousand years as one day." The time of storytelling is like the time of prayer. It is the time of the heart's longing. It is said of Einstein, "He was fearless of time and, to an uncommon degree, fearless of death."[57] As I live in the time of the heart's longing, in the time of prayer and of storytelling, I am learning to be less afraid of time, less afraid of death. As I go from living in my imagination like Don Quixote to facing death like Don Quixote on his deathbed, I begin to enter imaginatively into the love of God, to "realize" love, joining imagination and reality, and time begins to fade into love.

Time becomes ever more relative for me as I live in the time of prayer, as I live in the time of storytelling, as I live in the time of the heart's longing. "All the fear and misery her mother had suffered during the great war had passed her by," Grimm says of the little girl in his story, "and her whole life had been just one joyful moment." I learn through suffering, I should say, I learn through fear and misery, to live in that joyful moment, to live in the present, or rather to live in the presence of God, to live in the presence in the present, to live in the eternal moment. That is "the learning that comes of suffering"[58] that is spoken of in Greek tragedy, not learning simply to suffer but learning to live in the eternal moment, and in the inner light of faith learning to love.

What words, therefore, what music, what friendship goes into "living in love-longing"? There are "the words of eternal life" that go into the story of coming from God and returning to God. If the longing to which those words speak is put into music, it can be like the longing in Kierkegaard's prayers put into music by Samuel Barber or the longing that has passed in Leopardi's fragments put into music by Peter Maxwell Davies or the unrequited longing expressed in the serene melancholy of some of Mozart's music. If I go from living in my imagination to "living in love-longing," I can live in friendship like that of Don Quixote and Sancho Panza where friendship endures as I pass from imagination to reality, to an integration of imagination and reality, "realizing" love, and becoming caught up in the love of God. "One human heart goes out to another," I can say too, "undeterred by what lies between," undeterred by death and distance.

Between Heart and Heart

One human heart goes out to another,
undeterred by what lies between.

—Wilhelm Grimm

What lies between one human heart and another? All the divergence that takes place in the emergence of one human being and another, not to speak of the divergence that has taken place already in the emergence of the human race and its separation from other living beings. Our not understanding one another may be due in part to our not understanding other living beings, as may be suggested in the Grimm fairy tale of the young man who learned the language of the dogs, of the birds, and of the frogs. Once upon a time in story all living beings understood each other, but then human beings separated from the others, and now they are separated even from one another. One human heart therefore goes out to another, undeterred by this chasm.

Crossing the abyss between heart and heart is like going back to the beginning, going back to an original unity. Say I am a traveler, one who loves to be on a journey, who draws life from adventure, but I have a friend who is a dweller, who is at peace only at home and even on a journey is trying always to make a home wherever we are. When my own traveler's heart goes out to my dweller's heart, the part of me that is a dweller comes to life, the part that wants to find rest in my restlessness. Places in my heart come to life, places of peace and beauty, places of rest and dwelling, that allow me to understand my friend's heart. It is as if there were a place where once we lived together in peace and we are always trying to find our way back there again,

> Together we will take the road that leads into the West,
> And far away will find a land where both our hearts may rest.[1]

To understand each other, the dweller has to be willing to travel and the traveler to dwell, as we journey home together.

"We are unable to represent ourselves to ourselves, in order to choose between alternative selves,"[2] Richard Rorty says, trying to name the dilemma to which both Heidegger and Wittgenstein are speaking when they have recourse to the authority of language. If instead of choosing between alternative selves, the dweller and the traveler for instance, I am seeking to unite them or reunite them, I am passing from a sense of self as will to a sense of self as center of stillness. "We all have within us a center of stillness, surrounded by silence." I am going past language, as it were, to silence. What I come to, though, in this central place, is the silent place from which language comes. It is the place in me, I mean, from which I am able to understand others. To understand what another is saying I have to stop talking, but that is not enough if I remain in my will. I have to let go of my own will and move into my own inner quiet, I have not only to stop talking but to be quiet within myself. I have to listen in my center of stillness.

"We listen to our inmost selves and we do not know which sea we hear murmuring," Buber's saying, speaks of listening not just to others but to ourselves in our center of stillness. That was the point of departure in Buber's own thinking on "the road to I and thou." Maybe this center of stillness is the place from which language comes and the place to which language is directed. It is a point of arrival but also a point of departure. It is a place of "silence" and "stillness" but also a place of "murmuring." If "heart speaks to heart," let us ask, what does heart say to heart?

The Word at the End

Once there was a young man who seemed unable to learn anything, and so his father sent him away to study under great masters, but he returned saying he had learned from one the language of the dogs, from another that of the birds, and from another that of the frogs. At that his father disowned him, according to the Grimm fairy tale, but he was able to learn from the dogs of a buried treasure, from the frogs of his own destiny to become pope, and from the birds, two white doves, all that he must do and say as pope.[3] His story is not unlike that of Gregorius, "the holy sinner," according to Thomas Mann's retelling of that story, who also ended by becoming pope.[4] Learning the language of other living beings, going through sin to holiness, is learning to understand. If I am in touch with other living beings, if I am in touch with my own shadow side, I am able to understand other human beings, I am able to understand not only what is said but also what is unsaid in human language.

"We can know more than we can tell,"[5] Polanyi's saying, describes the mystery of language. Our emergence as the human race and our separation from other living beings has left a separation within us between what has emerged and we can tell and what has not emerged and we cannot tell. What has not emerged, our shadow side, is linked with other living beings and cannot be told insofar as we are unable to speak "the language of the birds" and of other living beings. Yet it is within us and we can know it. Of course we can speak of it as I am doing now, but that is not the same as speaking the language of other living beings. *What would it be to know the language of other living beings?* I think of the composer Olivier Messiaen and his use of bird songs in music.

In his *Quartet for the End of Time*, written and first performed when he was a prisoner during the Second World War, the third movement is a clarinet solo called "Abyss of the birds." Here is how Messiaen describes it in his introduction to the score:

> "Abyss of the birds." Clarinet solo. The abyss is Time with its
> sadnesses, its lassitudes. The birds are the opposite of Time;
> they are our desire for light, for stars, for rainbows and for
> joyful outpourings of song![6]

Although he studies bird songs very carefully and lets them sound very distinctively in his music, for instance in six pieces he wrote for piano in his late years, three based on the songs of the robin redbreast, and one each on the songs of the blackbird, the song thrush, and the skylark, he links them all with "our desire for light, for stars, for rainbows and for joyful outpourings of song." He links them, that is, with our longing. And in his last work, *Lights on the Beyond* (*Eclairs sur l'Au-Dela*), he has a movement entitled "The Lyrebird and the Bride-City," where the lyrebird of Australia is the symbol of "the soul which beautifies herself as a bride and goes forth to Christ, her husband."[7]

It is our longing for reunion that is expressed in "the language of the birds," it seems, "our desire for light, for stars, for rainbows and for joyful outpourings of song." That is our shadow side, when it is the unlived side of our life. The complexity of bird song, the complexity of musical language, suggests there is as much to what we cannot tell as there is to what we can tell in words. What is the relation between what we can and cannot tell? Is there some way of bringing together what we can and cannot tell to arrive at "the word beyond speech" that was in the beginning?

"It was the word beyond speech,"[8] the concluding sentence of Hermann Broch's novel *The Death of Virgil*, describing Virgil's final hours, speaks of Virgil coming to the point where words fail. It is a point where we pass from what we can tell to what we cannot tell. That point is always there on the edge of our telling, but to actually reach that point is like reaching a point of no return—Virgil at the end wanting to burn his *Aeneid*, Saint Thomas at the end saying he can write no more and all he has written is straw, Kafka at the end asking his friend Max Brod to destroy all his writings. "It was the word beyond speech" suggests it is rather a point of consummation, of fulfilment. Virgil wants to destroy the *Aeneid* but is persuaded not to destroy it, according to Broch, and comes to realize his words culminate in "the word beyond speech." He comes to that realization in four stages, as Broch tells the story, passing symbolically from water to fire to earth to air.

According to the ancient cycle of fire in Heraclitus, the sequence would be water, earth, fire, and air, as in MacDonald's story *The Golden Key*. Placing earth after fire, Broch puts a reversal into the story. "Water—The Arrival" tells of

Virgil's arrival by sea at Brindisi with the court of the emperor Augustus. Then "Fire—The Descent" describes the feverish thoughts of the dying Virgil. Then "Earth—The Expectation" tells mostly of Virgil's conversation with Augustus, Virgil wanting to destroy and Augustus to save the *Aeneid*. Finally "Air—The Homecoming" tells of Virgil's coming to peace and to "the word beyond speech." The reversal takes place in the conversation: instead of passing from fire to air, going up in smoke, the *Aeneid* is saved for the earth, and Virgil himself passes into the breath of spirit.

Does "the word beyond speech" lie between one human heart and another? There are moments of speech and moments of silence between friends. Do we pass through something like a cycle of fire in crossing the distance between us? There are times when the distance between us seems greater and times when it seems less. When it is greater, I feel I can rely only on God and not on human beings. When it is less, I am ready to trust in our friendship. Passing through fire is passing through those times when the distance is great. "But Jesus did not commit himself unto them," it is said in the Gospel of John, "because he knew all men, and needed not that any should testify of man: for he knew what was in man."[9] Such times are times of pain, though, not of cynicism, times of knowing the abyss between heart and heart. We cross that abyss then in conversation, passing over to one another, and we go from speech to silence then, coming back to ourselves. When "heart speaks to heart," we are trusting each other in spite of everything, and when we come then to silence we are ready for "the word beyond speech."

What comes then, as an artist friend of mine described it, after not painting for a long time, may be "some kind of deep, amorphous image of something either deep below the sea, or deeply in outer space, with a glowing, a soft glowing of what to me was the presence of the Holy Spirit of God, hovering, protecting all of the deep blue and deep green and deep violet." It is an image of presence. Or what comes, we could say, is a sense of presence. There is a word for this in biblical language and that is "I am," as the "I am" sayings of Jesus in the Gospels and especially in the Gospel of John. It is a word on the edge of speech when it is "I am" with nothing following, not "I am the way, and the truth, and the life" but simply "I am," not "It is I" or "I am he" as it is often translated but simply "I am."[10] It is on the edge of speech and seems to be an expression in speech of "the word beyond speech."

"It is for those who come here to fill the void with what they find in their center of stillness,"[11] Hammarskjöld says of the Meditation Room at the United Nations. What he says is true, it seems, also of the void between heart and heart. We fill the void with what we find in our center of stillness. If "the abyss is Time, with its sadnesses, its lassitudes," as Messiaen says, we fill it with "the birds" who "are the opposite of Time," "our desire for light, for stars, for rainbows and for joyful outpourings of song." We fill the void, that is, with our longing, we fill it with a sense of presence, of "I am," of "the word beyond speech." It is remarkable that Broch's *Death of Virgil*, like Messiaen's *Quartet for the End of Time*, was conceived in a Nazi prison camp. The words and the music are "for the end of time" while pointing back to the beginning of time. There is something eternal we are seeking in words and music, something beyond time, when one human heart goes out to another.

"Music must be treated as all things that are eternal, such as love and understanding, because it is these things that will carry us through the darkness of our lives and the death of our bodies to the moon of everlasting peace." These were the words of a Chinese grandmother to a friend of mine in a moment of frustration when the friend was trying to learn a difficult nocturne by Chopin. "You must love the music, not master it," the grandmother said. So it is too with words, we must love the words, not master them. By coming to words and music in this way, loving them and not mastering them, I come like Broch and Messiaen to "the end of time," to "things that are eternal such as love and understanding," as the Chinese grandmother said, "things that will carry us through the darkness of our lives and the death of our bodies to the moon of everlasting peace."

I can understand in this way "the authority of language" that Heidegger and Wittgenstein in their very different ways were recognizing. If I love the words, language has an authority for me it does not have when I master the words or try to master them. And music, if I love the music, not master or try to master it, is able to illumine the mystery of language that "we can know more than we can tell" by putting me in touch with what we cannot tell. Loving the words and the music sets me on my own journey through air and water and earth and fire to "the word beyond speech." We always live in a metaphor, it seems, just as we always live in a story, but the metaphor in which we live can change.

"In each period there is a general form of the forms of thought," Whitehead says; "and, like the air we breathe, such a form is so translucent, and so pervading, and so seemingly necessary that only by extreme effort can we become aware of it."[12] My education, I can see, has been in such a "form of the forms of thought" that is "like the air we breathe," and I have become aware of it only afterwards in passing over into other cultures and other lives and other religions and coming back with new insight to my own culture, my own life, my own religion. The point at which I became aware of the air I had been breathing, it seems, was when I began to use the phrase "passing over,"[13] or just before that, when I began to see my life opening up before me all the way to death, and in that light to see cultures and lives and religions in terms of their attitude toward death, passing over to them in virtue of that awareness, entering into their feelings and images and insights and ways of life and death.

Coming back to my own life after passing over, I find "We listen to our inmost selves," as Buber says, "and we don't know which sea we hear murmuring." I pass from air to water, from "the air we breathe" to the "sea we hear murmuring." Listening to that inner sea, I hear my heart's longing. What I don't know, listening to that murmuring, is my heart's desire. Is my heart's longing the love of God in me? If it is, my unknowing itself can be my way to God. There is a music in that murmuring, there are currents and drifts and streams, some of them warm, some of them cold, there are whale voices and other voices more mysterious, and there is oceanic consciousness that all are one. Even though I don't know which sea I hear murmuring, I know it murmurs of the oneness of all beings, and I know my heart's desire is union somehow or reunion. My not knowing my heart is an "unknowing in the which a soul is oned with God"[14] and oned with all souls. By unknowing, by unlearning what I think I know, I come into touch with the unknown.

And as I think of being oned with the unknown, I come to a peaceful place within myself, the center of the sphere of my life, the heart of my earth, as it were, and I pass from water to earth, from the "sea we hear murmuring" to "a center of stillness, surrounded by silence." It is not solid, though, but a hollow center, an empty center, like the inside of a hollow tree, and all the presence there is the surrounding silence. I take that as the presence of God, that surrounding silence, and the empty center I take to be myself, my deep self, for I inhabit that hollow place when I am at peace. Thus I have passed from telling to unknowing to silence. If "we can know more than we can tell," I am ready now to discover what we can know that is more.

I pass from silence to music then when my heart is kindled there in my center of stillness, and I look to music to know what is more than we can tell. I pass from earth to fire in the kindling of my heart. "Take this ring, Master, for your labors will be heavy; but it will support you in the weariness that you have taken upon yourself," the sage is told in Tolkien's trilogy. "For this is the Ring of Fire and with it you may rekindle hearts in a world that grows chill."[15] The kindling of my own heart enables me to rekindle the hearts of others, and the kindling and rekindling expresses itself in music. That is what music is, it seems to me, the language of the kindled heart, and that is what music does, "rekindle hearts in a world that grow chill."

Eternity, timeless existence, is what we can know in our center of stillness and, "surrounded by silence," cannot tell in words, and time in music is "a changing image of eternity." It is true, I am speaking in words now of eternity, and there are "the words of eternal life" in the Gospel of John, but as I come to these words, passing again from fire to the breath of air, I am conscious of coming to "the word beyond speech," of coming to the edge of music and words that has been called "the angel's cry." Michel Poizat uses that term, "the angel's cry," to describe the moment in opera when we are carried "beyond the pleasure principle," beyond the mere satisfaction of our expectations, to the experience of joyance (*jouissance*).[16] It is the experience of eternity in time, I want to say, the moment when we know presence in the present.

If we take that sentence, "We can know more than we can tell," and work out the relations in a cycle of fire,

we find our words lead us to realize our unknowing, and our unknowing takes us into our inner silence and our silence breaks out into music and our music issues into words of song. We have the passage from words through unknowing to silence in Wittgenstein's famous concluding sentence, "What we cannot speak about we must pass over in silence."[17] What is lacking in that sentence is the passage to music, for in music we find we can know and we can express what we cannot tell. All the same, "understanding a sentence is much more akin to understanding a theme in music than one may think,"[18] as Wittgenstein said later. There is a deep link between music and words, and there is a passage once more from music to words of song.

I believe this has been my own itinerary, passing from prose, through unknowing and silence, to music and poetry. Of course all of these exist at once and it is the human task, as Kierkegaard says, to unite all "the different stages of life in simultaneity."[19] If I take music as our key to "the language of the birds," if I take the way of music as our way of rejoining the other living beings that we left behind us long ago in our emergence as the human race, I begin to see myself how "understanding a sentence is much more akin to understanding a theme in music than one may think." I begin to understand words, that is, and the way of words in a new way, no longer as something separating us from other living beings, and I begin, like Virgil on his deathbed, to approach "the word beyond speech" that lies between us. Instead of burning the *Aeneid* I let the *Aeneid* stand, I let our words stand, that is, and I let our words speak to the heart.

Here are the words Messiaen lets speak in his *Quartet for the End of Time*, words of the angel in the Apocalypse with a rainbow around his head who swears "There will be time no longer!"[20] This is indeed "the angel's cry." Time emerges with our emergence and separation from other living beings, and it ends with our union or reunion with them once more. Or instead of saying that it ends, maybe we could say time ceases to be opaque and becomes translucent with eternity or even transparent to eternity. Whenever "heart speaks to heart," there is this translucency or this transparency, whenever "one human heart goes out to another, undeterred by what lies between." When I am listening to another person, knowing "We can know more than we can tell," and I let the words of the other speak to my heart, I come to understand not only what is told but also what is known, and thus the heart of the other speaks to my heart. The translucency or transparency here is like the relativity of time and distance in physics. We are "undeterred by what lies between," and so there is a meeting of hearts.

Passing through the cycle of fire to reach each other, though, we come again and again upon what we can know that is more than we can tell, upon "the angel's cry," upon "the word beyond speech." What if "the Word was made flesh, and dwelt among us"?[21] That would mean, after all our emergence and separation, we are on the road to union and reunion. Or it would mean at least that the road of union and reunion has opened up before us. For me, as an individual, emerged and separated, it would mean that my road is not one of further emergence and further separation but rather "the road of the union of love with God." Feeling my loneliness, my emergence, and my separation from other human beings as well as from other living beings, I am ready for union and reunion, and "the road of the union of love with God" sounds to me like the road of my heart's desire.

The Word in the Beginning

"The hint half guessed, the gift half understood, is Incarnation,"[22] T. S. Eliot says in *Four Quartets*. The hint, the gift is of union and reunion, after ages of emergence and separation. The hint is "half guessed," the gift is "half understood" because union and reunion is the direction we are not looking. The unconscious is the direction we are not looking while our consciousness is all of emergence and separation. Say I keep a diary. By keeping the diary I differentiate myself from my life, from the persons and the situations that belong to my life and enter into my life. I stand over and against my life as I record it in my diary, and so my consciousness is of my emergence and my separation. It may be that in my diary, as in Dag Hammarskjöld's *Markings*, the most frequent word is "loneliness." My loneliness, though, is my sense of being alone and of longing to be unalone, of longing really for union and reunion. So my differentiation from my life points on to a desired integration with my life, an integration that will mean reunion with humanity and union with God.

If I think of Incarnation, as T. S. Eliot does, as "the point of intersection of the timeless with time,"[23] then I am thinking of it as something we all have access to, for "We all have within us a center of stillness surrounded by silence." Whenever I come into my own center of stillness, "the hint" of Incarnation is "half guessed," "the gift" of Incarnation is "half understood." Among the hints and guesses is music, "or music heard so deeply that it is not heard at all," Eliot says, "but you are the music while the music lasts."[24] When I listen to music in my center of stillness, I am surrounded by a silence that allows me to hear the music rather than by a noise that would impair my hearing, or I am surrounded by a silence that allows me to be the music while the music lasts. I believe Eliot in writing *Four Quartets* was thinking especially of Beethoven's last string quartets, especially of the last one of all.

"Must it be? It must be! It must be!"[25] the words set to music in the last movement of the last string quartet, could be words becoming flesh. I mean the Grave of "Must it be?" followed by the Allegro of "It must be! It must be!" could be the expression of "the difficult resolution taken" to acknowledge the timeless in time. It is the movement from infinite resignation ("Must it be?") to faith ("It must be! It must be!"). Beethoven, always short of money, was owed some by a man named Dembscher. "Must it be?" were Dembscher's words when Beethoven asked for his florins. "It must be! It must be!" were Beethoven's words with a hearty laugh. And before using the words so seriously in a string quartet Beethoven used them jokingly in a round. But even in the quartet there is a passing from heaviness to lightness, from Grave to Allegro. To recognize the eternal in time is heavy at first with infinite resignation but is light in the end with the joy of faith.

Infinite resignation, if I may borrow Kierkegaard's term, occurs when one human heart is deterred from going out to another by what lies between. Faith occurs when "one human heart goes out to another, undeterred by what lies between." Infinite resignation occurs when we realize we are alone and we cannot make one another unalone. Faith occurs when we go out to one another, heart to heart, undeterred by our aloneness.

"You see, the brooks and the flowers and the birds come together," Grimm writes in his letter to the little girl Mili, "but people do not." He speaks to her of the distance separating people from one another and then he says nevertheless "one human heart goes out to another . . ." If one human heart goes out to another, I gather, it means rejoining the brooks and the flowers and the birds, rejoining all the living beings we separated from in our emergence, rejoining them while rejoining one another. So if infinite resignation means accepting our emergence and separation, faith means consenting to union and reunion. To go from infinite resignation to faith is to go from "the word beyond speech" to "the word made flesh." Thus Messiaen divides his *Quartet for the End of Time* in two, the first movements culminating in one of "Praise to the eternity of Jesus," praise to "In the beginning was the word," that is, praise to "the word beyond speech," and the last movements culminating in one of

"Praise to the immortality of Jesus," praise to Jesus risen from the dead, that is, praise to "the word made flesh." If I follow the music, I am carried on a cycle of fire from God to God, and if I follow closely enough, I learn something of "the language of the birds."

Passing over into this, I find myself not only listening to this music but also remembering bird songs I have heard myself, specifically one I heard long ago and put to music more recently in a song with words expressing the four states spoken of in the Upanishads: waking consciousness, dream, dreamless sleep, and oneness with God:

> O Wisdom, lead me
> from waking before you
> to sleep in your surrounding,
> and from finding rest
> to dreaming of you and me.
> and from dream to dreamless
> sleep together,
> and from one another
> to one.[26]

The angel's cry, on the edge of words, leads in this same direction, toward oneness with God and with all beings. As Messiaen conceives it, the angel's cry announces the end of time, the end of the time of our emergence and separation, I would say, and the beginning of our reunion or our return to the beginning in union.

Still, the consciousness we have gained in emergence and separation is retained when we begin looking in the direction we have not been looking. We are conscious of the contrast between the loneliness of emergence and separation and the joy of union and reunion, and so the reunion is conscious

in a way the original union was not. Messiaen expresses
the conscious contrast between the loneliness and the joy
in the contrast between "the Abyss" that is "time" and "the
birds," who are "the opposite of time." "Where Western
music since the Renaissance has drawn its progressive energy
from the asymmetries of the diatonic modes," Paul Griffiths
says, "Messiaen's music attains stasis by its use of modes that
reduce distinctions among their constituent notes," and "the
removal of distinctions obscures the arrow of time."[27]

I see the symmetry Griffiths speaks of, obscuring the
arrow of time, also in the bird song I wrote above. Perhaps
this harmonic symmetry is native to the time of other living
beings, as it is to the more primordial forms of human
time where human life is integrated more with the cycle of
the seasons, spring and summer and fall and winter. I think
of the harmonic symmetry of the pentatonic scale used in
folk songs around the world. As I come into this symmetric
time out of the asymmetric consciousness of emergence and
separation, it strikes me as an answer to the death that has entered our consciousness with time's arrow. "Humans perish
because they cannot join the beginning to the end,"[28] Alcmaeon said. Coming into cyclical time out of time's arrow,
however, I learn to join the beginning to the end in a way that
subsumes the arrow of time, seeing everyone and everything
coming from God and returning to God. The asymmetry
of time's arrow from past to future is subsumed into the
symmetry of love's direction from God to God. The past
deepens into the process of coming from God and the future
into that of returning to God.

Here the direction is not greater and greater wakefulness,
ending in utter sleeplessness, "how could anyone hide from
that which never sets?"[29] It is rather like the direction in the

Upanishads from waking consciousness, to dream, to dreamless sleep, to the One. Awakening, nevertheless, coming to consciousness, is the essential thing in the emerging sense of "I." "We have learnt that unconscious mental processes are in themselves 'timeless,'"[30] Freud says in *Beyond the Pleasure Principle*. Time seems related with waking consciousness, timelessness with dream and dreamless sleep and the One. Yet we experience timelessness when we are in our "center of stillness, surrounded by silence," and we are awake then all the same. These states of dream and dreamless sleep and the One, I surmise, can be enacted or reenacted in our center of stillness, and this conscious enactment of timeless states is what is being sought in the Upanishads, and is the conscious realization of our union and reunion with one another and with all living beings.

Waking consciousness thus is the last phase of emergence and separation and the first of union and reunion. Incarnation, as it is understood in Christianity, means the infinite significance of an individual, Jesus of Nazareth, and thus the infinite significance of each and every individual in their relation to this one. "If you believe, you will understand,"[31] Saint Augustine says. If I believe in this one individual, Jesus of Nazareth, I come to understand something of myself and of all others, I discover my inscape and I discover the inscape of every other person as well, I discover the infinite significance of myself and of everyone else. That is an insight, particularly at this time when the sheer number of people in a crowded world has grown so large that the individual seems insignificant, a time when people very commonly feel unnecessary and superfluous. Inscape, as I am thinking of it here, is what is symbolized by "the new name"[32] in the New Testament, when Simon becomes Peter and Saul becomes

Paul. It is the inwardness of the individual, the inner landscape that is illumined by the light of the Incarnation. It is
what comes to light when I myself enter into the unconditional relation of Jesus with God.

Dreaming, the second phase in the Upanishads, when
it is consciously enacted or reenacted in our center of stillness, becomes a discerning between true and false images
that appear on our inner landscape. According to Virgil in
the *Aeneid* there is a Gate of Horn and a Gate of Ivory:
true dreams and visions come through the Gate of Horn,
false ones come through the Gate of Ivory.[33] When C. S.
Lewis was arguing his way from doubt to faith, he was saying
"myths are lies, even though lies breathed through silver."[34]
Tolkien in an all-night session with Lewis was arguing that
myths rather are shadows of the true story, and the true story
is that of Incarnation. "All tales may come true," Tolkien
wrote later; "and yet, at the last, redeemed, they may be as
like and as unlike the forms we give them as Man, finally redeemed, will be like and unlike the fallen that we know."[35]

Dreamless sleep, the third phase in the Upanishads, when
it is consciously enacted or reenacted in our center of stillness, becomes a finding of inner peace. "And in his eyes
there was peace now, neither strain of will, nor madness, nor
any fear,"[36] Tolkien says of Frodo, his main character, at the
end of his trilogy. This is the happy ending, as in fairy tales,
but as it comes true in the story of the Incarnation. Peace is
sought and found in all the great religions, but in the story
of the Incarnation we come through suffering to peace, as
Frodo does in Tolkien's story, through suffering and even
through moral failure, as here where Frodo succumbs to the
spell of the Ring's power at the end and then is saved from
himself by Gollum, an otherwise evil figure in the story. I

think again of Saint Augustine returning to God with tears. It is peace, therefore, as in all the great religions, and yet not simply detachment, but it is a peace we come to through tears.

Oneness or the One, the fourth and final phase in the Upanishads, called Atman or God dwelling in us and corresponding to Brahman or God at large in the universe, is our experience of the presence of God. When it is consciously enacted or reenacted in our center of stillness, it is felt as the silence surrounding our center, as in that saying "We all have within us a center of stillness surrounded by silence." The "I am" sayings of Jesus, I have learned from my friend David Daube, express the Shekinah, the presence of God among us.[37] And I gather from the Gospel of John that we too can say "I am": when the blind man, having received his sight, acknowledges Christ, he says "I am," and when Peter denies Christ, he says "I am not."[38] When I enter then myself into the unconditional relation of Jesus with God, I too can say "I am," letting those words interpret the silence surrounding me in my center of stillness as the presence of God.

When one human heart goes out to another, therefore, we can say "I am" to one another, as it were, as we tell our stories to one another, speaking "from the heart," as Beethoven says of his Kyrie Eleison, "may it go to the heart." "I am" is the word of eternal life that opens the way between heart and heart. Antonio Machado, a poet who fled Spain during the Civil War, wrote,

> I love Jesus who told us
> heaven and earth will pass.
> When heaven and earth have passed,
> my word will still remain.

> O Jesus, what was your word?
> Love? Forgiveness? Charity?
> All your words were
> one word: Awake![39]

I think the one word is "I am." It does awaken us to our own "I am," and we find ourselves telling our own stories in this consciousness, like Saint Augustine writing his *Confessions* and inventing the genre of autobiography, and we find ourselves coming like him through tears to inner peace and to an awareness of the great "I am" of the presence of God.

As I follow Saint Augustine's steps, I find he goes from his own story to the larger story in which we all live. He ends his *Confessions* with reflections on memory and time and the beginning of time, and then later in *The City of God*, after debating with those who blame Christianity for the fall of Rome, he proceeds to tell the larger story with its beginning in the beginning of time, its middle in the present, and its ending in the ending of time. Why doesn't he continue to speak heart to heart with God in *The City of God* as he spoke in his *Confessions*, heart to heart with God and therefore heart to heart also with us? I suppose it is because the story he has to tell is of epic proportions like the *Aeneid* of Virgil, because he is telling of the City of God as Virgil was telling of the City of Rome, because he has therefore to speak like Virgil in "the second voice of poetry," as T. S. Eliot calls it, where the poet is addressing an audience, instead of "the first voice of poetry," where the poet is engaged in a soliloquy, letting himself be overheard by others.[40]

When he does broach this larger story in his *Confessions*, nevertheless, speaking at the end about the beginning of time, he gives us a taste of what it would be to tell the larger story heart to heart. He reads the scriptural account of the beginning, letting it speak to his heart and letting his heart speak in response, and in the narrative of the beginning he finds the ending, when God rests on the seventh day after creating the world. He sees eternal rest in that rest, the rest he spoke of in the beginning of his *Confessions*, "our hearts are restless until they rest in you." I think of T. S. Eliot writing in his *Four Quartets*, "In my beginning is my end" and "In my end is my beginning."[41]

"In my beginning is my end," as Eliot understands it, means to remember death, *memento mori*, but "In my end is my beginning" means to remember eternal life, to live toward life rather than death. To know my end is in my beginning is to know I will die someday—that is the knowledge that estranges us human beings from other living beings, it seems, and even from one another insofar as death singles us out of the crowd. To know my beginning is in my end, on the other hand, is already to know the language of other living beings, "the wave cry, the wind cry, the vast waters of the petrel and the porpoise." It is to know "another intensity," as Eliot says, "a further union," "a deeper communion."[42] It is *a conscious enactment or reenactment of the unconscious unity of being*. We come to "the wave cry, the wind cry," the fire song, the earth song, in coming to union and reunion with God and with one another. We come, in a simple way I believe, to a universal communion.

This conscious enactment or reenactment of unity, I mean, is "the natural prayer of the soul: attentiveness. And in this attentiveness," as Walter Benjamin says, are "included all living creatures, as saints include them in their prayers." I think of Saint Francis of Assisi and his Canticle for Brother Sun, where he praises God for "Brother Sun" and

"Sister Moon" and "Brother Wind" and "Sister Water" and "Brother Fire" and "Mother Earth" and last of all for "Sister Death-of-Body."[43] Messiaen weaves this canticle into the eight scenes of his one and only opera, *Saint François d'Assise*, a late work, where the high points are the fifth scene, "the angel musician," and the sixth, "the sermon to the birds" where the singing is followed by what Paul Griffiths calls "Messiaen's grandest bird concert." As Saint Francis dies in the last scene, he prays, "Music and Poetry have led me towards you: by image, by symbol and by want of Truth . . . Deliver me, intoxicate me, dazzle me forever by your excess of Truth."[44]

So what we come to by waking consciousness and by conscious enactment or reenactment of dreaming and dreamless repose and oneness is not yet that "excess of Truth" but only an attentiveness that is "the natural prayer of the soul," an attentiveness that can express itself in music and poetry. We go out to one another with a sense of infinite significance, telling stories that may come true in forms like and unlike the ones we give them, telling of joys and sorrows recollected in tranquility, speaking out of a surrounding silence that may be the very presence of God. And we find ourselves going on from our own stories to the larger story in which we all live, finding its beginning in that unity of all beings of which we have become conscious.

"We can know more than we can tell," and our knowing can be expressed in music, I conclude, and "Music must be treated as all things that are eternal, such as love and understanding," as the Chinese grandmother said, "because it is these things that will carry us through the darkness of our lives and the death of our bodies to the moon of everlasting peace." And if we go like Messiaen from "the word beyond speech" to "the word made flesh," we come to see the eternal in us as a veritable life incarnate in us. Incarnation seems to mean essentially that the story comes true, the song comes true, the heart's desire is actually fulfilled. It is true, the story is still a story, the song is still a song, the desire is still a desire. "God dazzles us by an excess of Truth," Messiaen's angel sings. "Music transports us to God by its want of Truth."[45] Still, if we believe in and hope for the fulfilment of the heart's desire, then "what lies between" heart and heart seems to drop away and "one human heart goes out to another, undeterred." Faith, it has been said, is "seeing light with your heart when all your eyes see is darkness."[46] Our times are dark times in the isolation of one human being from another. Let us see what it would be therefore to see light with your heart in the darkness and isolation of our times.

This World's a City
Full of Straying Streets

This world's a city full of straying streets,
And death's the marketplace where each one meets.

—Shakespeare and Fletcher

"Various are the roads of humankind," Novalis writes. "One who follows and compares them will see strange figures emerge, figures which seem to belong to that great cipher which we discern written everywhere, in wings, eggshells, clouds and snow, in crystals and in stone formations, on ice-covered waters, on the inside and outside of mountains, of plants, beasts and humans, in the lights of heaven, on scored disks of pitch or glass or in iron filings round a magnet, and in strange conjunctures of chance."[1] Human ways are like paths on the surface of a sphere, like meridians on an earth that is round: they diverge from one another until they pass the equator, and then they converge. While they are diverging, human beings are emerging and separating from one another, and "strange figures emerge," but when they begin to converge, a unity begins to appear, and the many figures "seem to belong to that great cipher which we discern written everywhere."

What is that great cipher? When our paths are diverging and we are emerging and separating, we all seem to be heading for a horizon. Are we heading simply for death? When we pass the equator and our paths begin to converge, we seem to be heading for a union or reunion. Are we heading for eternal life? If we follow and compare the emerging and separating paths, we do indeed come upon "strange figures." I think of the strange figures that emerge in the words and the music expressing these ways in our times, Jazz, Blues, Soul, Country, Rock, Metal. It is illuminating to consider these ways of music as ways of life and death, to let them answer the question "If I must die someday, what can I do to fulfil my desire to live?"[2] Each of them poses the question in its own way, and each answers in its own way, expressing a vision of life and death. If I pass over into them, letting words sing to my heart, letting music resonate in my soul, I come back with new insight to my own way of life and death, and I begin to discern the great cipher.

I remember learning jazz clarinet as a teenager, taking lessons from a very good jazz clarinetist and even playing with him at times on the local radio. Jazz was always somewhat foreign to me, though, and my love was rather for the classical music I was learning on the piano. Improvisation is the essence of Jazz, and passing over into it means entering into improvisation as a way of living. "*Music as a state of being,*" Charles Hartman says in *Jazz Text*, "as in the day-long or week-long festivals held by the Berbers and other tribes, exercises a quite different power over its listeners, *means* in a quite different way, from (in Susanne Langer's phrase) *music as symbolic form.*"[3] For me to pass over into Jazz from the classical music I love is to pass over from music as symbolic form to music as a state of being. I wrote a song about this:

Why begin? Why end?
Why not go on and on?
Life is a timeless festival,
and we who improvise are playing,
and the music is a state of being
and not just symbolic form,
but we who sing and listen come and go,
and my song does begin and end,
attention is my prayer of soul,
and here is my beginning and my ending,
where I am,
inside a song.[4]

There is an answer to death in "music as a state of being" just as there is in "music as symbolic form." The one answers death with life as a state of being just as the other answers death with life as symbolic form. I think of Shakespeare's words in the play he began and Fletcher finished, *Two Noble Kinsmen*, "This world's a city full of straying streets, and death's the marketplace where each one meets."[5] Let us consider the ways of life expressed in "music as a state of being" and "music as symbolic form," and let us consider their meeting in the marketplace of death.

The Way of Music as a State of Being

Jazz, Blues, Soul, Country, Rock, and Metal are indeed "straying streets, and death's the marketplace where each one meets." What is it like to walk these straying streets towards death? A blues singer, Son House, when asked why he waited until adulthood to become a blues singer, described his religious conversion, how when "a young teenager and up like that I was more churchified," how he used to ask himself "Is there—this one time I'm just gon see is—is any way to get this thing religion they goin round here talkin about, puttin on and goin on?" and how he went out alone one night:

> I was there in that alfalfa field and I got down. Pray. Gettin on my knees in that alfalfa. Dew was fallin. And man, I prayed and I prayed and I prayed and for wait awhile, man I hollered out. Found out then. I said, Yes, it is somethin to be got too, 'cause I got it now![6]

If "attention is the natural prayer of the soul," I wonder if this is what is being expressed in his singing? *Does music express the natural prayer of the soul?*

There is music and music, some does, some does not express the attention that is the natural prayer of the soul. There is some that expresses rather a pursuit like Arthur Rimbaud's of the "systematic derangement of the senses"[7] with its ecstasy, its approach to madness, its yearning towards death, its rapture of the senses. These are like two ends of a spectrum, attention the natural prayer of the soul at one end and systematic derangement of the senses at the other, and along this spectrum we can arrange Jazz, Blues, Soul, Country, Rock, and Metal. Passing over into attention the natural prayer of the soul is something I am ready and willing to do, but the thought of passing over into the systematic derangement of the senses is something that takes me aback.

I get an idea of what it is to pursue the systematic derangement of the senses simply by reading Rimbaud's prose poem *A Season in Hell*. Over the entrance of Dante's Inferno there is the famous inscription, "Abandon all hope ye who enter here."[8] Dante enters imaginatively into hell but does not abandon hope. That is the difference here. Rimbaud enters hell by abandoning all hope. I begin to see a way of passing over into Rimbaud's hell of derangement of the senses without having my senses deranged and that is to enter it in Dante's fashion, to enter imaginatively but without abandoning hope. That will allow me to come back from passing over, to go on from Inferno to Purgatorio to Paradiso as I pass along the musical spectrum, but also to come back from the whole thing with new insight to my own way of life and death. That is how I understand "passing over," as an imaginative entering into another way that allows me always to come back again to my own way. It is one thing to pass over; it is another to be converted.

"A journey is a fragment of hell,"[9] Muhammad's saying, true as it is of being lost in a desert or being caught in a sandstorm, is true also of an imaginative journey such as the one I am contemplating here. But then again "to be lost in the desert was to find one's way to God,"[10] and my imaginative journey can become like Dante's a journey through hell and purgatory to heaven, a divine comedy. "Music," it has been said of the aboriginal songlines in Australia, "is a memory bank for finding one's way about the world."[11]

There is an African love song I have come across that consists of only one lyrical sentence:

I walk alone.[12]

When I came across it in a collection called *The Unwritten Song* by Willard Ropes Trask, it brought me to a halt. It made me begin to realize and to think out the connection between love and loneliness. I think of it again here because it is simple, because it is elemental, because it can express the loneliness that is without hope in hell, that combines with hope in purgatory, that becomes love in heaven. Let us imagine what this song would be in Jazz, Blues, Soul, Country, Rock, and Metal. There are words and music here, and the words can go through transformations of meaning along with the music on each of these straying streets. Let us imagine the music while actually working out the meaning of the words along each way. There has to be an openness in the music to allow for improvisation, but the words can give symbolic form even to music as a state of being.

Imagining Jazz is imagining something very similar to the meditative thinking we have been doing here, improvising on a theme. There is another element in Jazz besides improvisation, though, and that is "voice," as when we speak of someone finding his or her "own voice."[13] In fact, in all of these modes, Jazz, Blues, Soul, Country, Rock, and Metal, there is this element of "voice" and much is made of "who's who" among musicians. There is a sense of "I," that is, on each of these ways that is expressed in "voice" along with a sense of life and death that is expressed in improvisation. There is the person who lives the life and there is the life that is lived. If I try to find my own voice in Jazz, I am trying to find myself in music as a state of being. Maybe that is why I pulled back from it as a teenager. I wasn't at home in music as a state of being. Now if I take those words "I walk alone" as a theme for Jazz, I am taking words that are very expressive for me and I am letting them express a state of being in which I live. To do that I have to be willing to be in that state of being, willing to walk alone. I do walk alone, but am I willing to walk alone?

If I am unwilling, the words "I walk alone" can express a deep melancholy, can be an appropriate theme for Blues. I think of Ornette Coleman's jazz version of "Lonely Woman"[14] and the contrasting vocal version where the melody is altered rhythmically to become a blues line with its standard twelve bars. I take the jazz version to be an expression of willingness to walk alone, the blues version to be an expression of unwillingness to walk alone. The musical difference is that the jazz version is instrumental, the blues version vocal, but also the jazz rhythm is free, the blues rhythm measured. "My music doesn't have any real time, no metric time," Coleman says. "It has time, but not in the sense that you can time it. It's more like breathing, a natural, freer time . . ."[15]

Time, even measured time, is essential to Blues. When I "have the blues" or am "feeling blue," I am living in the sorrow of time while longing to live in the joy of "a timeless festival." Gospel is to Blues as a sacred motet is to a secular madrigal, as eternity is to time, and people pass over from the one to the other. "When I was growing up in the South," blues singer and songwriter and guitarist B. B. King says, "you sang Gospel in church on Sunday and Blues on the back porch every evening."[16] If I am alone and unwilling to walk alone, I am not living in a No to my life. I am living rather in a Yes to the deep longing in my loneliness. So Gospel is to Blues not as Yes to No but as eternal love to human longing. Blues can express both of the elements in loneliness, the sense of being alone and the longing to be unalone. It is when the longing is filled with hope that comes of faith in eternal life that Blues turns to Gospel. Time is linked with the deep loneliness of the human condition. Timelessness is linked with our dearest hopes of union and reunion.

"Soul grew out of the fusion of the Blues with Gospel,"[17] it has been said. Certainly it brings an element of hope and confidence to the unrequited longing of Blues. Still, the hope in Soul is thisworldly, and that in Gospel is otherworldly, though the impression and feeling of hope in Soul comes especially from the work of Ray Charles and Sam Cooke "reworking Gospel stylings to create a whole new art form" and "carving secular Soul from Gospel traditions."[18] When I am feeling "the transcendence of longing," how my longing always goes beyond anything I have, I see the point of a transcendent hope, a hope that reaches beyond this life to a life after life, and that is the hope in Gospel. Yet I wonder at the same time if there is not something in this life, beyond the life I know, to be sure, but still within this life before death, that can be my heart's desire, and that is the hope in Soul.

"What is Soul?" Ben E. King asked in a song, and he answered "Soul is something from deep inside."[19] I think of the distinction between "self" and "soul" where "self" is linked with the life I am living and "soul" is linked with my unlived life. Thus the hope in the music called Soul is to live that life hidden deep inside that I have not lived. Soul the music is "an amalgam of uninhibited Gospel stylings and secular Blues themes," and it is said "Dig into the background of most great soul artists and you will find they started out singing in church."[20] There is a turning here, a conversion, not to faith dissolving life into the eternal but vice-versa to a dissolving of the eternal into life, deriving "style or will" from faith but "situation or emotion"[21] from life. Those are Max Jacob's terms for the two elements of poetry. Here "style or will" comes from Gospel, and "situation or emotion" comes from Blues. Still, there are soul artists like the Staple Singers who are able to go back and forth between Gospel and Soul. So the turning need not be a conversion but can be a passing over that allows a coming back.

"Country is white man's blues music,"[22] B. B. King said, and it is true, "situation or emotion" in Country is very similar to that in Blues, and it is very Country to sing "I walk alone." The difference is in "style or will." Here too the style comes not only from folk music but also from hymns, like "Amazing Grace" and "'Tis a Gift to be Simple." And here too singers go back and forth between the sacred and the secular like singers in the Golden Age of Song in the Renaissance going back and forth between the motet and the madrigal. The hope in "I walk alone," if there is hope, is always "to walk with you," and that can be a prayer, "to walk with you, my God," or a love song, "to walk with you, my love." A love song can become a prayer, and a prayer can become a love song, as heart sings to heart.

"If you are ready to leave father and mother, brother and sister, and wife and child and friends, and never see them again," Thoreau says, "—if you have paid your debts, and made your will, and settled all your affairs, and are a free man, then you are ready for a walk,"[23] and Thoreau is speaking of walking alone. There is something like that also in walking with God, leaving everyone and everything behind to walk with God. And there is something like that in walking with another human being in love. I can see in these words of Thoreau the lyrics of many sacred and secular songs of Country, not that they derive from his words but that they express this letting go of everyone and everything to walk alone, to walk with God, to walk in love. If I consider writing lyrics myself, however, I have to decide if I am willing to let go of everyone and everything, and for what. To walk alone? To walk with another? To walk with God? If it were to walk alone, I would be giving myself to a life of thought. If it were to walk with another, I would be giving myself to a life of feeling. If it were to walk with God, I would be giving myself to the life that arises out of my center where thought and feeling meet.

But why must I let go of everyone and everything? I suppose it is because I must become heart-free if I am to find
my heart's desire. "You must deny yourself! Deny yourself!
That is the everlasting song,"[24] Goethe's Faust complains.
Rock is the opposite of "the everlasting song." It sings rather
of the hope and the desire to experience life to the full, to
have bliss, to have your heart's desire without having to let
go of everyone and everything, without having to become
heart-free. When I think of all I am missing in life, the way
of Rock can seem tempting, to go for a fullness of life, to
"go for it." What I have learned, though, about "infinite
grace," how the road not taken can rejoin the road taken,
seems a different and better answer. Instead of "going for it,"
according to this, I do take a road and give up other roads,
but I can hope for a fullness of life nonetheless by "infinite
grace."

"Lord Ronald," Stephen Leacock says in one of his *Nonsense Novels*, "flung himself upon his horse and rode madly
off in all directions."[25] I imagine a man on a horse breaking
up into many images galloping away from each other. If I do
try to take all roads, to ride off in all directions, I can walk
them or ride them only in my imagination, and so imagination becomes all important in Rock, especially in Psychedelic
Rock. Living in my own imagination, I can see what this
means, apart from any use of psychedelic drugs. What then
is Rock? Jazz takes the typical musical form of "melody /
string of solos / melody."[26] When there is a "fusion" of Jazz
and Rock the solos tend to disappear. "A fusion performance reabsorbs solos into complex, virtuosic ensemble playing,"[27] or when the solos are retained, instead of being a
series of brilliant improvisations, they tend to become, as
blues and rock guitarist Eric Clapton put it, "endless, mean-

ingless solos."[28] When I try to take all roads, even though it is only in my imagination, I am trying somehow to rejoin humanity, to know all human possibilities. Even if I am playing solo, I am trying not to be solo, not to be isolated. I am trying to walk, but not alone.

When you seek to walk all roads, however, or to ride off in all directions, or to have all human experiences, you find that some human experiences are dark and destructive. Metal is the music of these dark experiences and of the longing for death. Here we do find Rimbaud's pursuit of the "systematic derangement of the senses." Certainly we find the ecstasy, the approach to madness, the yearning towards death, the rapture of the senses. If Freud is right and we long not only to live and to love but also to die, there is something in us that can resonate with such music. "Appetite for Destruction," "Welcome to Hell," "Hear Nothing, See Nothing, Say Nothing," "Kill 'Em All," "Let's Go Crazy,"[29] and such like titles of albums and songs suggest the gallows humor of Metal. Is humor a saving grace here?

There is a deep connection between sexuality and mortality, and the connection can be felt strongly in adolescence when sexuality emerges in power. The appeal of Rock and Metal has been especially to teenagers, and the mixture of sexuality and death in the themes of Rock and Metal seems to be the very mixture the teenager feels, expressed with the power of loud music. Passing over into such music arouses the adolescent in the adult. The humor of the music seems to be adolescent humor, the humor of a person who is trying on masks and laughing at the grotesque in the mirror. Rimbaud too wrote *A Season in Hell* when he was quite young and then left poetry behind him to go on a journey of experience that left him ultimately exhausted and sick and disillusioned. As I pass over into such a journey myself, thinking of my own journey in later life, I can see how I have been going back and forth between such a journey of experience and a voyage of discovery. When I seek to experience all of life, I am seeking to have lived, as if life could be exhausted, but when I seek rather to discover, I am going on a voyage into the unknown, as if the mystery of life were inexhaustible.

If life is inexhaustible, it makes sense to let go of having and trying to have, to let go in order to be heart-free and heart-whole, and to find heart's desire in openness to the mystery of life. "Aristotle's premise that a work must have a beginning, middle, and end, which can seem trivially obvious to us, was not obvious before his time,"[30] Hartman says in *Jazz Text*. Perhaps it is the point of Jazz that life is inexhaustible, without beginning or end, "Life is a timeless festival, and we who improvise are playing," even though "we who sing and listen come and go, and my song does begin and end." So then, if I must die someday, what can I do to fulfil my desire to live? I can join in this timeless festival, I can improvise, I can sing, I can listen. What is more, "attention is my prayer of soul, and here is my beginning and my ending, where I am, inside a song." I join in by attention, by prayer, by song.

Inexhaustible life, without beginning or end, is divine, and joining in the timeless festival means being caught up in a life that is light and love. I am caught up humanly in life and light and love, humanly because "we who sing and listen come and go, and my song does begin and end." As my teacher, Bernard Lonergan, said,

> It is as if a room were filled with music, though one can have no sure knowledge of its source. There is in the world, as it were, a charged field of love and meaning; here and there it

reaches a notable intensity; but it is ever unobtrusive, hidden, inviting each of us to join. And join we must if we are to perceive it, for our perceiving is through our own loving.[31]

It is by loving that I come to realize there is love in the world, by loving, by attentiveness to human beings and to all living beings, by attention, that is, "the natural prayer of the soul." Music here is a state of being, as in tribal festivals, as in Jazz. It is not itself the loving, the attentiveness, but an expression of the love, an expression of the attention. My own reluctance towards Jazz, my not feeling at home in music as a state of being, may be a sign of my reluctance to join the timeless festival, to join in the pervasive love, to join at all and thus somehow to lose my autonomy, to lose my independence.

"Melody / string of solos / melody," the musical sequence of Jazz, suggests there is room, nevertheless, for solo existence in this joining and participation. If I am not mistaken, it is an existence that comes of willingness to walk alone, a *willingness* to walk alone, I say, that welcomes companionship, not a *will* to walk alone that excludes company. I think again of Frodo in Tolkien's trilogy, how at each great turning point in the story he has to be willing to walk alone, but how each time he finds companionship after all. Participation in life and light and love, as I understand it, means being caught up in life and light and love, or willingness to be caught up, or even willingness to walk alone in life and light and love, but it also means sharing life and light and love with one another, or willingness to share with one another, or the welcoming of companionship.

My song "I walk alone," therefore, if I imagine it as a song in Blues and Country, is a song of unrequited longing, of lack and loss and letting go. In Soul and Gospel it is a song of longing filled with hope in this world (Soul) or in another world (Gospel). In Rock and Metal it is a song filled with the will to be unalone. In Jazz it is a song of willingness to walk alone, to improvise and to solo, that nevertheless welcomes companionship. I see in Jazz thus a hint of an ongoing reality and of personal participation in an ongoing reality. Still, in all of them I see music as a state of being that expresses a state of being in life, a will, a hope, an unrequited longing, a willingness in the face of death. What I look for rather in music as symbolic form is an expression of the autonomy I am always afraid of losing in joining in music as a state of being. And I look also for an expression of the "infinite grace" or mercy I have seen as an alternative to riding "madly off in all directions."

The Way of Music as Symbolic Form

Autonomy and Mercy,[32] the title of Ivan Nagel's essay on the operas of Mozart, states a dilemma of music as symbolic form. Autonomy is the independence of the human person, the freedom to choose a path in life, forsaking all others. Mercy is the infinite grace of God who can give us not only what we have chosen but also what we have forsaken. We can celebrate autonomy in music, as Mozart does in *The Magic Flute*, or we can celebrate mercy, as he does in his *Requiem*. These were the two great compositions he was working on at the end of his life. Symbolic form, as we know it in classical music, was emerging at the same time as the idea of human autonomy. Mozart was celebrating human autonomy in music at about the same time as Kant was formulating the autonomy of reason and of conscience in philosophy. Yet

Mozart was also celebrating mercy, an idea that goes back in music to the polyphony of the Golden Age of Song in the Renaissance and beyond that to the purity and simplicity of plainsong. What happens in classical music is that autonomy and mercy, however opposed they seem to one another, come to exist side by side.

It is true, "infinite grace," giving us not only what we have chosen but also what we have forsaken, is a reformulation of mercy over and against autonomy. What is more, the freedom to choose a path in life, forsaking all others, is a reformulation of autonomy. As Kant conceived it, the autonomy of reason was the legislative power of reason to impose order on our experience, and the autonomy of conscience was the legislative power to impose order on our behavior, the freedom to choose the principle on which we act. The "categorical imperative,"[33] according to Kant, was simply to act on principle. The freedom to choose the principle on which we act becomes then the freedom to choose our path in life. Say I act on the principle of loving "with all your heart." That means finding a path in life on which I can be wholehearted.

I have taken the phrase "forsaking all others" from the formula of betrothal in the Book of Common Prayer (1559), "And forsaking all other, keep thee only unto her, so long as ye both shall live?"[34] I use it to bring out the sense of a road taken and of a road or roads not taken in choosing a path in life. If we walk one road, we have in effect forsaken other roads, and we can be haunted by a road we have not taken. There is a strong sense of choice like this also in composing music, and in classical music there is a sense of imposing form, like autonomous reason imposing form on experience. I don't mean to imply that Kant had any influence on music but only to say that he comes out of the same matrix as classical music. To be sure, the forms imposed can seem so universal and necessary that the choice exercised in imposing them can seem inevitable. When the freedom of the choice is felt, though, and the forsaking of other possibilities is conscious, then there can be room beside autonomy for something like mercy restoring us to a fullness of life.

Symbolic form is expressive form in language and myth and in the arts, and is like the form given to our experience by our reason, or again like the form given to our life by our conscience. That is how Ernst Cassirer understands the term, I believe, in his *Philosophy of Symbolic Forms.*[35] Autonomy thus is of the essence of symbolic form, but mercy is a challenge to symbolic form, for mercy is an expression of what is greater than ourselves. Still,

> The quality of mercy is not strain'd,
> It droppeth as the gentle rain from heaven
> Upon the place beneath.[36]

And the quality of music too, expressive of what is greater than ourselves, is not strained, even within the limits of symbolic form.

I think of Mozart's *Ave Verum,*[37] written in the last summer of his life, where mercy comes to pure and simple expression within the limits of symbolic form without any apparent strain. The words, celebrating the presence of Christ in the Eucharist, are in effect an answer to the loneliness of the song "I walk alone":

Ave verum	Hail true
corpus natum	body born
de Maria virgine,	of Mary virgin,

Vere passum,	Suffered truly,
immolatum	immolated
in cruce pro homine,	on the cross for humankind,
Cujus latus perforatum	Whose side was pierced
unda fluxit	and flowed with water
et sanguine:	and with blood:
Esto nobis	Be unto us
praegustatum	a foretaste
in mortis examine.	in the passage of our death.

I notice there are some words at the end of the original plain-song,[38] words perhaps too pious, that are left out in Mozart's setting of the song:

O Jesu dulcis!	O Jesus sweet!
O Jesu pie!	O Jesus kind!
O Jesu fili Mariae!	O Jesus Mary's son!

Leaving these words out, Mozart's setting ends more starkly on the note of death. Still, there is a warmth I can feel in Mozart's version. If I compare Mozart's with the *Ave Verum* of Josquin des Pres, composed two centuries earlier in the Golden Age of Song, as I have been calling it, I could say of Mozart's, borrowing some words of Tolkien, "less keen and lofty was the delight, but deeper and nearer to mortal heart."[39] If I were to compose an *Ave Verum* now, two centuries after Mozart, what would I want it to express? The "delight" in Josquin's is indeed "keen and lofty," and that in Mozart's is indeed "deeper and nearer to mortal heart." But our loneliness has become more acute, I believe, in these last two centuries, and our sense of "real presences" has become more tenuous.

Real Presences,[40] as George Steiner calls them in his book, are an answer to our loneliness, the real presence of other persons, the real presence of God, even the real presence of Christ as sung in the *Ave Verum*. Our loneliness has become more acute as we have become more conscious of autonomy, and our sense of real presences has become more tenuous as we have become less conscious of mercy. Still, loneliness itself becomes love, or the longing in loneliness becomes love, as if hunger were to become bread. This bread is like the waybread that Tolkien speaks of that gives strength but does not satisfy desire. The presence of Christ that is celebrated in the song is like this way bread. "It did not satisfy desire," Tolkien says of the waybread, and yet it "had a potency that increased as travelers relied on it alone and did not mingle it with other foods. It fed the will, and it gave strength to endure, and to master sinew and limb beyond the measure of mortal kind."[41] Real presence here is presence to our longing, presence to our loneliness.

If I try and compose an *Ave Verum* now, therefore, I will be seeking to express a sense of real presence to the longing in our loneliness. Instead of setting the Latin words or my translation of them, let me try an interpretation, playing on the words "alone" and "all one":

All one
with us
in body birth,

All one
with us alone
in suffering,

Alone
with us all one
in dying,

Be with us
then when
we are alone,

Jesus
with us
in body and in blood.

I find I can sing these words to the melody of the plain-song (in the last stanza I have to repeat "Jesus with us" twice for "O Jesu dulcis! O Jesu pie!" before singing the entire stanza for "O Jesu fili Mariae!"). I am singing here of the loneliness we feel in suffering and in facing death. Suffering drives us into ourselves, and the more intense it is the more difficult it is for us to feel what others are feeling, so intense are our own feelings. Death singles us out, as Heidegger says, and it is when we are facing death that we are most alone. Christ himself felt abandoned on the cross. And so we pray him to be with us in our loneliness, the alone with the alone, alone becoming all one. It is true, Heidegger thought there could be no sharing, no "being with" (*mitsein*) in the facing of death.[42] I want to say, on the contrary, we share in our loneliness, we share in our human condition of mortality and suffering, and we can be with one another even when we are most alone.

I find I can sing the words of my *Ave Verum* also to Josquin's melody, the plainsong in slow motion, as it were, but in two and three voices. I remember singing Josquin's motet years ago in a choir, though I believe we sang only the first part, the first two stanzas.[43] Singing my own words to this slow-motion melody in one voice after another, I find myself savoring the words, savoring "all one," the old expression from which "alone" is derived, hinting at the oneness in aloneness. Also I savor the repeating words "with us," suggesting Emmanuel, "God with us." The slow motion of the melody is of course the style of polyphony, allowing one voice to move against the background of another in counterpoint, but it has the effect of contemplation.

I find I can sing my words also to Mozart's melody, repeating the words of each stanza to fit the music, dropping my last stanza as Mozart drops the last stanza of the original, and ending on the note of aloneness as he ends on the note of death. Singing my words "then when we are alone" to his melody for "in mortis examine," I think of our aloneness in the face of death, I think of the times I have assisted people on their deathbed, holding their hand maybe and yet sensing their aloneness, their knowing they are dying while others go on living. I think of spiritual friendship in my life now and know I too will be alone in my own death, am alone now facing the prospect of my death. I see Heidegger's point more clearly, feel it more vividly I should say, but I see and feel also the point of faith in "God with us." Mozart repeats the phrase "in mortis examine" with climactic music at the end. Repeating "then when we are alone" to that music turns "Be with us" into a cry, an outcry.

If I look for such a cry or outcry in music now, two centuries after Mozart, I think of Stravinsky's *Symphony of Psalms*.[44] I find I can sing my "Be with us" to his "Laudate," and my "All one with us" to his "Alleluia." Those are the words that are most memorable in the music, "Laudate" and "Alleluia" in the last movement, and so those are the phrases that stand out most as I sing through the music with my own words, the imperative "Be with us" and the indicative "All one with us." I can divide my lyrics into three parts as in Josquin's motet, the first two stanzas, then the next two, and then the last, repeating as needed, to go with Stravinsky's three movements. The phrases "Be with us" and "All one with us" are then repeated in the last movement along with the last stanza. I feel the inadequacy of my words in such a grand setting, and yet I feel the reality of the prayer.

Mercy is the theme of the words Stravinsky is setting from the Psalms, "Hear my prayer, O Lord . . ." and "Waiting, I waited on the Lord . . ." and "Alleluia! Praise the Lord! . . ."[45] Autonomy seems to have been swallowed up in mercy as I have moved from plainsong to Josquin to Mozart to Stravinsky. Still, I have something of an experience of autonomy here in composing lyrics and setting them to existing music. If I go on now and compose music of my own for my lyrics, I experience autonomy all the more. Say I write the music for two voices singing *a capella*, men and women singing in responsive alternation and with the women's voices leading. Say I take the first four notes of the plainsong and continue it myself for the first two stanzas, using a pentatonic scale and a rhythm of four eighth notes against a half note and against two quarter notes and increasing the compass of the melody to an octave and a third; then I take the first four notes of the second theme in the plainsong and continue it in a similar way for the next two stanzas; and then I repeat the first melody for the last stanza.

Simplicity itself is the result, and a kind of serenity. It is very simple counterpoint, in effect a round at the octave. When autonomy is a theme, as in *The Magic Flute* (I think of the opening chords), it contrasts more strongly with mercy, "the sovereignty of the One," as Ivan Nagel says, "is supplanted by the freedom of the individual."[46] When mercy is a theme, I am finding, autonomy appears rather in the creative process of composing words and music. Mercy appears

All One

Andante   John S. Dunne (1994)

too, nevertheless, in the element of inspiration in the creative process. When I am composing lyrics or composing music, I am exercising autonomy, choosing words, choosing melody and rhythm and harmony, but I feel I am discovering rather than inventing the words and the music, discovering as if I were inspired, my heart kindled and my mind illumined.

There are songs whose form is strict, like Shakespeare's sonnets, and there are songs whose form is rather more free, like Shakespeare's songs from the plays. Invention here is *inventio* in Latin, actually discovery, not the sheer construction that invention has come to mean in English. Whether I am working with strict form, like the round or canon in my composition in two voices, or with free form, like the free verse of my lyrics, I am engaged in the kind of invention that is discovery, not in the kind of invention that is just construction. Bach's Two and Three Part Inventions are two and three part discoveries. If I seek to invent, to construct, to be purely original and exercise a perfect autonomy in composing, I become paralyzed; I cannot write, I cannot compose. If I seek rather to discover, I seek and I find, I find relationships between words, I find relationships between tones, I find relationships between words and music.

Discovering relationships, my heart is kindled and my mind is illumined. The kindling is the enthusiasm, the illumining is the light of *Eureka!* "I have found it!" The kindling of my heart and the illumining of my mind is my experience of grace, my experience of mercy. I find my way in words and music by following the guidance of my heart. The kindling of my heart with enthusiasm leads to the illumining of my mind, showing me which way to go among the many possibilities of words and music that open up before me. There are ways taken and ways not taken, but I do not simply choose the ways I take, I discover them rather in the kindling of my heart, and the discovery is itself the illumining of my mind.

Many ways of words and music open before us now after many years of experimentation in the twentieth century. "One who follows and compares them will see strange figures emerge," as Novalis says of human ways generally, "figures which seem to belong to that great cipher which we discern written everywhere . . ." If I follow the guidance of my heart, I find myself looking always for "that great cipher." At the beginning of the century, with the coming of atonal music, the larger forms of sonata and symphony based on tonal relations became unworkable and there was a return to the simple forms of song and dance. A cycle of songs, Schoenberg's *Pierrot Lunaire*, and a cycle of dances, Stravinsky's *Rite of Spring*, became the models of music. Now at the end of the century, though there has been a return to tonal music as well as the discovery of atonal relations like tonal relations, I find myself looking for "that great cipher" in the simple forms of song and dance.

A song cycle, nevertheless, and a dance cycle can have the quality of larger symbolic forms. Consider Shakespeare's songs from the plays, not intended to be a cycle, and consider his sonnets, written as a sequence.[47] All the same, if I take the songs as if they were a cycle, I make some discoveries. One thing is the songs are madrigals, not motets; secular, not sacred songs, and yet they deal with life and death, and I can discern in them "that great cipher" I am seeking. The same is true of Mozart's arias from the operas. The other thing is the cycle, if I set the songs to music, looking to "that great cipher," comes to have a transcendent meaning. It becomes a cycle of mystical songs.

I think of Stravinsky's setting of songs from Shakespeare, where three magical songs become three mystical songs. One is "Music to hear" from the sonnets; another is "Full fathom five," Ariel's song from *The Tempest;* and the other is "When daisies pied" from *Love's Labour's Lost.*[48] These three magical songs become mystical songs, I want to say, because of the feeling of timelessness in the music. It is like the sense of timelessness in Messiaen's music that makes his cycle of dances, *Quartet for the End of Time*, a cycle of mystical dances. Messiaen in his *Technique of My Musical Language* speaks of the modal harmony and the complex rhythm he uses to create "that sort of *theological rainbow* which the musical language, of which we seek edification and theory, attempts to be."[49] I think of the modal harmony and the free rhythm of plainsong, a differently modal harmony and a differently complex rhythm that also creates a feeling of timelessness, as if to show how eternity is not tied to any one musical technique.

Time is "a changing image of eternity" in Mozart's *Ave Verum* with its shifting harmony, shifting with each stanza and coming to climax at the end with the thought of death. Eternity is here as a serenity and simplicity in the shifting of time and as a resolving of death's poignancy in harmonic peace. After listening to atonal music, I find the tonal relations here all the more distinct. "Be unto us a foretaste in the passage of our death" ("Esto nobis praegustatum in mortis examine") speaks to me or sings to me more clearly than ever. Time and eternity meet in the thought of death, and the agony of death is resolved in peace. All is foretaste, nevertheless, a foretaste of death, a foretaste of peace, a foretaste of eternal life.

The Meeting of the Ways

Alone on the way of music as a state of being, all one on the way of music as symbolic form, I meet myself at the crossroads. I am coming back to myself from passing over. It is the reverse of Lord Ronald flinging himself upon his horse and riding madly off in all directions. So in passing over I have been doing the very thing I have ascribed to Rock, going off in all directions in my imagination. And now I am coming back to reality in myself but with new insight from my encounter with music as a state of being and music as symbolic form. Now after saying eternity is not tied to any one musical technique, I find myself studying Messiaen's technique in depth. What is the language of eternity? All the ways meet in death, according to Shakespeare, "And death is the marketplace where each one meets." Can I learn the language of eternity at the meeting of the ways? Meeting myself at the crossroads, I learn the language of "I am" and "I will die."

  "Being toward death," as Heidegger describes human existence, can become "being toward life" for me, I believe, or "being toward eternal life," if I can learn the language of eternity. Instead of living with the thought of death as my end, I can live with the thought of death being a part of my life, an event of my life like birth. "Death is not an event of life," Wittgenstein says. "Death is not lived through."[50] If, on the contrary, death *is* an event of life like birth, then death *is lived through* and is not simply an end. Music is a language,

or can be a language, I believe, in which death is encom-
passed by life, is taken up into life as a state of being or into
life as symbolic form.

If "we can know more than we can tell," music can express
what we can know and cannot tell of the mystery of life and
death. "As death, when we come to consider it closely, is the
true goal of our existence, I have formed during the last few
years such close relations with this best and truest friend of
mankind, that his image is not only no longer terrifying to
me, but is indeed very soothing and consoling!" Mozart
wrote to his father during his father's last illness. "And I thank
my God for graciously granting me the opportunity (you
know what I mean) of learning that death is the *key* which unlocks the door to our true happiness." Mozart was able in
his *Requiem* to express all those feelings, "terrifying" and "no
longer terrifying" and "soothing and consoling." If I understand him rightly here, though, when he says "death is the *key*
which unlocks the door to our true happiness,"[51] he is saying
death is indeed an event of life which we live through into
eternal life and happiness, something he says at the end of the
Ave Verum in words and music.

We can know death is an event of life, we can know death
is lived through, I believe, in a way we cannot tell in words
alone but only in words and music. Considering just the way
we speak of death without having died, Wittgenstein con-
cluded "Death is not an event of life. Death is not lived
through." Considering the way we sing of death, on the other
hand, "we think caged birds sing, when indeed they cry,"[52] as
John Webster says, and we think we sing of death, when
indeed we cry. Yet crying of death, we can know more than
we can tell just speaking of death, for in singing that is crying
there is all of us and more than there is in just speaking.

It is by dwelling in the particulars of our life that we can know more than we can tell. If I say "I walk alone," I am saying I am alone on my journey in life. If I sing "I walk alone" as a love song, I am singing of my longing for a companion on the way. And if I sing "All one with us . . . ," I am singing of a sense of presence with us on life's way. My indwelling in the particulars of my life can reach therefore to a sense of being alone and beyond that to a longing to be unalone and beyond that to a sense of presence. When it comes to death, my song can carry a sense of being alone in the face of death, of longing to be unalone, and even of a foretaste of life in death. When Mozart lay dying and his wife's sister Sophie came to his bedside, he said "Ah, dear Sophie, how glad I am that you have come. You must stay here tonight and see me die." She tried to persuade him he would not die, but he replied "Why, I have already the taste of death on my tongue."[53] Did he have also the foretaste he prayed for in the summer in his *Ave Verum*, the foretaste of eternal life?

Spending his last days composing his *Requiem*, Mozart was certainly thinking in those days not only of death but of eternal life. I suppose that is the point of music as symbolic form, to embody the symbols such as eternal life that answer to the primal questions of our state of being such as loneliness and death. I don't mean to say music as symbolic form is aimed at music as a state of being but only to say it does answer to our state of being and its questions. I think of Blues, for instance of a song called "Death Is Awful,"[54] where we have the raw question that something like the *Requiem* answers. It is true, the question itself is transfigured in music as symbolic form, and death passes from the "awful" to the sublime.

"Deep loneliness is sublime, but in a terrifying way,"[55] Kant says. There is in the sublime, as he observes afterwards in his critical thinking, an element of "boundlessness." There is indeed something boundless about deep loneliness, a boundless longing, and there is something boundless too about death, an opening onto infinity. That is how death appears in Mozart's *Requiem* and generally, it seems, in music as symbolic form. If we consider a small work, though, such as the *Ave Verum*, the sublime, which is large, according to Kant, passes into the beautiful, which can be small. Here death "is not only no longer terrifying to me, but is indeed very soothing and consoling," though there is an echo at the end of its having once been "terrifying." In this small motet then "death is the *key* which unlocks the door to our true happiness." Small is beautiful, and great is sublime, because death is truly an event of life, because death is lived through, because death opens onto infinity.

I think of still another *Ave Verum*, that of William Byrd,[56] written in the century before Mozart, where death is not an issue so much as real presence. That was the controversy of Byrd's time: Is it real presence or only symbolic presence? That becomes another question for us: Can music as symbolic form convey real presence or can it convey only symbolic presence? Byrd's motet, perhaps his best known and most loved work, is written in the "familiar" style of polyphony where the rich changing harmony outweighs the counterpoint, and it conveys a vivid sense of presence. In Mozart's motet then the rich changing harmony becomes more purposive and more melodic and conveys a sense of movement in time, of life's movement toward death, and of the mystery of passage through death to life.

Real presence is like "realization" in music as symbolic form, the vivid imagination of something that is real. If I take one more step with the *Ave Verum* and envision the kind of motet Anton Webern composed on Latin texts, I come to an insight into the realization of presence and how it bears upon the loneliness of death. Webern was the twentieth-century master of the musical miniature, and his Latin motets were brief canons for soprano with clarinet and with bass clarinet.[57] If I try the Latin words "Ave verum corpus natum . . ." with his atonal melodies, setting each one of the five stanzas to one of his five short canons, I find I cannot keep to his method of one note to one syllable. Then I realize the words he has already set to the music are similar to the words I am trying to set. There is a motet about the Mother and the Child (2), three about the Cross (1, 3, 5), and one about mercy (4). What is missing among the themes is the Eucharist. What comes out in the atonal melodies is the humanness of Christ and his agony and the sense of "God with us" in the agony of human existence. There is an intensity that is also a simplicity.

This simple intensity, this intense simplicity can show me the way. My own motet in two voices, "All one with us . . . ," if I recast it in a form like Webern's for soprano and clarinet or for soprano and bass clarinet, has the simplicity but lacks the intensity. I can see the direction I have to take in life and in music, not to lose simplicity but to gain intensity, to encompass somehow the conflict of life in the peace of the presence, to bring the passion into the peace. I can see how the loneliness of death belongs to the conflict of my life, while the realization of presence belongs to the peace. Speaking of the loneliness of death, Heidegger says, "The less one is in a hurry to steal away unnoticed from this perplexity, the longer one endures it, the more clearly one sees . . ."[58]

As I ponder all the hopes and fears of my life that are not taken into my inner peace but are left outside in a kind of outer darkness, I wonder if they all devolve upon the loneliness of death, the hope of being loved and known, the fear of being unloved and unknown. "Devolve" is the right word here because they belong to the loneliness of love and pass into the loneliness of death when my life opens up before me all the way to death. Once when I had pneumonia and the thought of dying rose up in my mind, I thought of the scene from the life of Saint Thomas Aquinas as he lay dying, listening to the Song of Songs. That is the way to die, I thought, listening to the Song of Songs, Solomon's song of the lover and the beloved. That is the way to live too, I thought, caught up in the love of God. That is the only love that is great enough to take up into itself the loneliness of love and the loneliness of death. The loneliness is already upon me, my hopes and my fears are upon me, but if I can pass through the loneliness to the love of God, I can pass through death already to life, to being in love with God.

"Only a bird knows how to die,"[59] Czech poet Jaroslav Seifert says in his cycle of rondels, *Mozart in Prague*. I've seen birds die and fall headfirst upon the grass. A bird lives and makes music right up to the end, then simply dies. A human being doesn't just live and die but always has a relationship with life and with death. Still, when you awaken to the love of God, you become like a bird alone, like a sparrow, Saint John of the Cross says, commenting on the verse of a psalm, "I awakened and became like a sparrow all alone on a house top."[60] I see here the willingness to walk alone that I saw also in Jazz. There it was a willingness to solo and yet to participate in an ongoing musical reality. Here too it is a willingness to walk alone and yet to participate in a reality that is greater than ourselves, a willingness to walk with God.

"Listen to the birds. They are great masters,"[61] Messiaen says, quoting his teacher Paul Dukas. To live and make music right up to the end is wisdom, we can say too; it is to walk with God. Still, just as bird song changes and becomes human in our music, there is a consciousness and a willingness about walking humanly that makes it a knowing and loving walk, and that leads us beyond falling headfirst upon the grass in death. "Are not two sparrows sold for a farthing? and one of them shall not fall on the ground without your Father," Christ says in the Gospel of Matthew. "But the very hairs of your head are all numbered. Fear ye not therefore, ye are of more value than many sparrows."[62] There is a sense of being loved and valued here that leads to being able to love. There are two elements in loneliness: the sense of being alone and the longing to be unalone. It seems both elements carry over into the love of God, the sense of being alone becoming the sense of "I" in the "I and thou" of love, and the longing to be unalone becoming the longing for union or reunion with God, for "I in thee" and "thou in me."

If I listen to the Song of Songs recited, as in the French film *Therese*,[63] or if I read it through myself, I can hear in it that sense of being alone and that longing to be unalone. I realize it is a cycle of love songs that have become mystical songs. What if I were to take the love song "I walk alone" as a mystical song about the love of God? I suppose it would become an expression of living in my center of stillness where "alone" is always changing to "all one." I can see the answer to my question about the hopes and fears I have left outside my inner peace is to bring them with me into my center and let them be changed into peace. It is to let my peace become a simple intensity, an intense simplicity. It is a matter of being there myself in my entirety with all my hopes and fears, "being there" (*Dasein*) in the presence of God.

As a mystical song "I walk alone" is the song of one who is "like a sparrow all alone on a house top." Such a sparrow has five properties, according to Saint John of the Cross: "it ordinarily perches in the highest places"; "it keeps its beak turned in the direction of the wind"; "it is ordinarily alone"; "it sings very sweetly"; and "it has no definite color."[64] If I sing the mystical song "I walk alone," I am walking on high ground, according to this, in the direction of the divine wind, alone, singing, and without the color of any human obsession or compulsion. Saint John of the Cross puts the aloneness very strongly: "it is ordinarily alone and will have no other bird whatsoever near it, so that, when any other perches beside it, it flies away." I want instead to make my distinction between a will to walk alone that excludes all company and a willingness to walk alone that welcomes companionship. All the same, it is true that even when we share the spiritual journey, as in a spiritual friendship, there is still an inner journey we have to go alone.

There is an aloneness in loving God "with all your heart, and with all your soul, and with all your might" and not dividing your heart between God and someone or something else. It is the aloneness of all oneness. You find yourself being weaned from your human relations. It is still true, when I am heart and soul in love with God, I am able to be heart and soul in all my human relations and I am capable of spiritual friendship, of sharing the love of God with another person. Yet I am alone, not that I have God to myself, but I am all one in loving God and in the ins and outs of love with God. When we are spiritual friends, we are like Mossy and Tangle in *The Golden Key*, alone at first in coming each from our own origin, then together on the journey, then alone on our own inner journey, then together at journey's end.

"I walk alone" expresses the natural prayer of the soul, therefore, when it becomes a mystical song. It expresses the aloneness that is all oneness, the attention that is love "with all your heart, and with all your soul, and with all your might." I have been treating words such as "I walk alone" as if they had music in them. That was truer in ancient Greek and Latin, where verses were composed of words in quantitative rhythm, each syllable having a rhythmic value, long or short. But there has been a separation between words and music, as Georgiades says in *Music and Language*,[65] ever since rhythm shifted from the quantitative value of syllables to accent. Making use of that separation, I have imagined the words "I walk alone" set to different kinds of music and my own words "All one with us . . ." sung to different melodies. Now I can imagine love songs becoming mystical songs, as in the Song of Songs or the poetry of Saint John of the Cross, and I can see that is the direction my life has also to go. *Love songs can become mystical songs when they encompass the loneliness not only of love but of death.*

"Deep loneliness is sublime, but in a terrifying way," Kant's saying, points to a way that is terrifying but a way also on which "perfect love casts out fear."[66] As I read the poems of Saint John of the Cross, I can see the deep loneliness in his "Dark Night of the Soul" and I can see the perfect love that casts out fear there and in his "Living Flame of Love."[67] A mystical song is one that sings of deep loneliness, one that sings of love that casts out fear, one that carries us from loneliness to love. Kant's own instance of deep and terrifying loneliness is the story of a loveless man whose hell is to live in utter aloneness.[68] It is the paradox of mystical song to know heaven is that same loneliness changed to love, to know there is a secret passageway from hell to heaven, from loneliness to love.

A mystical song is words, a mystical dance is music that can take us from time to timelessness ("There is time in hell," Aquinas says), and the words can be set to the music. "I am in great unrest," Eowyn says in Tolkien's trilogy, and Faramir, who comes to love her, "saw that she was hurt, and his clear sight perceived her sorrow and unrest."[69] Here is another meaning the song "I walk alone" can have, it can mean "I am in great unrest," and I can begin to resolve my unrest just by expressing it in words and in music. "It was a time of sitting with my aloneness . . . ultimately strengthening but very painful," as a friend of mine said of living in the unrest of loneliness. If we associate restlessness with time, we can associate rest with eternity or timelessness. To pass from restlessness to rest is to experience aloneness as "ultimately strengthening." Perhaps that is what Saint Augustine means when he says "our hearts are restless until they rest in you," they are restless as aloneness is "very painful" until they rest as aloneness becomes "ultimately strengthening."

"There is time in hell," Aquinas's saying, can seem very true when you are sitting with your aloneness, resting in your unrest. "In hell there is not true eternity," he says actually, "but rather time."[70] Time becomes "a changing image of eternity" then as aloneness becomes all oneness, as it becomes "ultimately strengthening." As I study Messiaen's technique for expressing the sense of eternity in music, I find it consists largely in "the charm of impossibilities,"[71] as he calls them, rhythms that cannot be reversed without changing back into themselves, modes that cannot be transposed more than a few times without changing back into themselves. Yet he does not look for melodies that cannot be reversed without changing back into themselves. So the forward movement of time is still there in melody.

What is more, melody has the primacy, according to Messiaen, over rhythm and harmony.[72] Our movement from time to eternity likewise leaves time intact and we come not to pure eternity but to time full of eternity. So the forward movement of time is still there in mystical song. Only time's arrow from past to future becomes love's direction from God and to God. Thus in passing from love song to mystical song I do not leave human love behind so much as find it in the love of God. The forward movement of my loneliness is there in my longing for union with God, and my loneliness for other human beings is there in my longing for our reunion in God. I think of a friend's dream of alcoves where we would be together again in the afterlife and of the spiritual friendship we have already in this life. As I sing "I walk alone" I am on my way from living in my presence to myself to living in the presence of God with us, "All one with us . . ." Alone is on the way to all one.

The Road of the
Union of Love with God

He used to say there was only one Road;
that it was like a great river: its springs were
at every doorstep, and every path was its
tributary.[1]

—J. R. R. Tolkien

If the roads not taken in life do indeed rejoin the road taken, then it makes sense to speak, as Tolkien does, of "the Road," and to say "there is only one Road," and to imagine the "straying streets" of Shakespeare meeting not just in the marketplace of death but in the road that "goes ever on and on." This road, I believe, is the mystic road, what Saint John of the Cross calls "the road of the union of love with God."

There are two nights that occur along the mystic road, according to Saint John, "the night of sense" and "the night of spirit."[2] As I understand it, "the night of sense" is the experience of grace coming through the empty places of a life, and "the night of spirit" is the experience of divine love taking the place or places filled until then by the human justification of a life. There are empty places in a life, that is, and full places. Say there are places left empty by love and places filled by work in my life. I never realized how lonely I was, I mean, until love entered my life and I began to experience the mystery that "shows itself and at the same time withdraws" in a human relationship, the ebb and flow of love and friendship. I experience a kind of fullness in my work, on the other hand, writing out of the emptiness and longing I feel in love and friendship, giving expression to it in words and music. Writing and composing seem to give rather than take energy, to put me in touch with my unrequited longing as if it were a source of energy.

When I come to the poetry of Saint John of the Cross then, I want to interpret it in terms of the longing of the human heart. But I learn from his prose that his poetry is really about the pure love of God. To pass from the longing of the human heart to the pure love of God is to go through "the night of sense" and "the night of spirit." That experience of grace coming through the empty places of a life, of divine love replacing the human justification of a life, is already there in our lives, I believe, is already there in my life, trying to happen, but is not welcome. To make it welcome then is to pass from the longing to the love. "Love is the reality," Broch's Virgil comes to realize, "and what he had held to be love was only yearning,"[3] but the yearning can become the love.

Let us see how yearning turns to love in "the night of sense" and "the night of spirit" that occur on love's road. "Your path is poetry," Broch's Virgil is told on his deathbed, "your goal is beyond that of poetry."[4] Our path is words and music, I want to say, our goal is beyond that of words and music. Let us see how the way of words and the way of music and the way of spiritual friendship come together on "the road of the union of love with God."

The Night of Sense

I enter a kind of night of sense on the way of spiritual friendship when I enter a period of withdrawal, an ebb tide of the human relationship. Say my friend withdraws, draws back from me for whatever reason, and I am left with a feeling of distance instead of our former intimacy. It is true, the mystery, the element of the unknown in life, "shows itself and at the same time withdraws" in our relationship just as it does in other aspects of life. So there is something more fundamental going on here than the "good reasons" or the "real reasons" for my friend's withdrawal. I am dealing not just with my friend but with the mystery of life. I am dealing somehow with God. If I am willing to deal with the mystery, to deal with God here, I enter into what Saint John of the Cross is speaking of as "the night of sense." I can give expression to it myself in words and music, and if I do so I find an affinity with his words and with the words and music of others who have entered willingly into the dark night. I find there is something universal in my experience.

Here is my translation of the first three stanzas of the poem "Dark Night" by Saint John of the Cross, the only stanzas of the poem he comments on in prose:

In dark night
with longings kindled into loves
—O lucky venture!
I set out unseen,
my houschold now at rest.

In darkness and in safety,
by the secret ladder, in disguise,
—O lucky venture!—

in the shadows and in hiding there,
my household now at rest.

In the lucky night,
in secret so nobody saw me
and I saw no thing,
with no light no guide other
than that burning in my heart.[5]

He uses the same stanzas over again for his discussion of "the night of spirit." The rest of the poem is about the meeting of the lover and the beloved, "the union of love with God." So the night of sense and spirit is the passage to union with God, and Saint John of the Cross spends his prose talking about it rather than the union of love itself because he is at pains to help people who are making the passage.

Being one of those trying to make the passage, I am much more aware right now of my starting point than I am of my goal. I think of Roland Barthes speaking of "night" (*nuit*) in *A Lover's Discourse*.[6] He seems to have in mind a starting point like mine, a period of withdrawal, an ebb tide in a human relationship. He doesn't leave the starting point, though, but wants to use mystical language simply to illumine the darkness of human relations. For me the essential thing is to go from the human relationship to a relation with the mystery that shows itself and withdraws, to enter into a relationship with God. That means a kind of releasement, a letting be (*Gelassenheit*) towards the things I expected in the human relationship, and an openness to the mystery showing and withdrawing. That sets me at peace with the human relationship, if I can indeed let be and be open to the mystery, "my house being now at rest," and it allows me to climb down "the secret ladder" and set out unseen and unseeing except for the light "burning in my heart."

"God sensible to the heart,"[7] Pascal's definition of faith, *Dieu sensible au coeur*, could also be a definition of "the night of sense." What is light to the heart is night to the senses—the inner light is darkness to our ordinary perceptions. It is this inner light, I believe, that can carry us through the darkness of our lives to wisdom rather than resentment in old age. Let us see if it can also carry us through the troubles of love to union with God.

"I experience alternately two nights, one good, the other bad," Barthes says. The good night is when "I am here, sitting simply and calmly in the dark interior of love." The bad night is when I am troubled by the ebb tide of the human relationship, when "I am in the very darkness of my desire,"[8] of my unrequited longing. There is a direction in that good night, I want to add to what Barthes says, a direction that can lead me directly into the mystery of life. "Love is a direction and not a state of soul,"[9] Simone Weil's saying is a warning to me, not to be discouraged at the experience of the bad night nor to stop at the experience of the good night, states of soul, but to follow love's direction into the heart of the mystery. When "I am here, sitting simply and calmly in the dark interior of love," then "my household is at rest," and I am ready to climb down "the secret ladder" and to follow the light "burning in my heart." If love is a direction and not a state of soul, I ask myself now, *what is love's direction?*

"The love is from God and of God and towards God,"[10] the words of the old Bedouin to Lawrence, have been my guide on love's direction. If I place them in this context of "The Dark Night of the Soul," they suggest that the night is from God and of God and towards God, that the night itself can guide me to God. The stanzas that follow in the poem "Dark Night" speak of the guiding light and the guiding night:

> It guided me
> more surely than noonday light
> to where awaiting me
> was someone I knew well,
> there where no one appeared.
>
> O guiding night!
> O night more lovable than dawn!
> O night uniting
> love with loved one,
> changing her into her love![11]

When I am in the ebb tide of a human relationship, I experience mostly the bad night that Barthes describes, "when I am blinded by attachment to things and the disorder which emanates from that condition." Barthes says he experiences mostly the bad night. "Most often I am in the very darkness of my desire," he says; "I know not what it wants, good itself is an evil to me, everything resounds, I live between blows, my head ringing."[12] Can love's direction be discerned even in the bad night? I believe it can be discerned if I can let go of the state of soul I am experiencing, if I can let go of the sadness, the anger, the desperation, the despair I am feeling. But then if I let go of the sadness, I pass into the good night. I remember a wise old nun in Manaus telling me something like this about the people I was meeting on the Amazon. "They seem happy," I said to her. "Are they really happy?" "They can be sad for a day," she replied, "but they can't hold on to sadness."[13] It is possible to "hold on to sadness," I gather, and it is possible to let go. If I can only let go of sadness, like these people, I can discern love's direction.

Letting go of sadness seems to go with looking in the direction I have not been looking. "The unconscious is the direction we are not looking,"[14] it has been said. Say I have been looking to my friend for my fulfilment, but now I turn in the direction of my life itself, time's arrow from the past into the future, hoping to find something more than just time's arrow. To look in that direction for my fulfilment is to trust that I am being led, being guided and guarded, even though I seem just now to have lost touch with something very essential to my life, this friendship that I prized. "Subtle is the Lord God, but not malicious,"[15] Einstein said. To believe in that is to enter into a relation with the mystery itself that shows itself and withdraws. The mystery! That is it! The unconscious direction we are not looking! The direction we are usually looking is to other human beings. To turn from them to the mystery itself is the secret of letting go of sadness, to turn to the mystery in faith.

Dios lo quiere, the thing simple wise people say on the high plain of Bolivia and Peru when something sad happens, "God wills it," seems to be the simple secret of letting go of sadness. For as *quiere* also means "loves," there are overtones of love in *Dios lo quiere*. Just the sound of the words in Spanish makes me think of the words in English, "God cares." If I can believe "God cares," I can let go of sadness. I can say, as in the Grimm fairy tale recently discovered, "God and my heart are weeping together."[16] I think of the music of Górecki, especially his *Symphony of Sorrowful Songs*, and especially the second song using words of a graffito written on a cell wall of a Gestapo prison by an eighteen-year-old girl:

> Little mother, do not cry,
> Pure Queen of Heaven,
> Be always with me,
> Hail Mary![17]

Here, as it were, "Mary and my heart are weeping together." Letting go of sadness ("do not cry") is possible because of a sense of being unalone ("be always with me"), a sense of "I am with you."

"God sensible to the heart" can take many shapes, that of God caring, *Dios lo quiere*, that of the sorrowing Mother, as in all three of the Sorrowful Songs of Górecki's Symphony, and that of Christ the beloved of the soul, as in the poetry of Saint John of the Cross. The Christian Trinity, according to the Koran, is God, the Mother, and the Son, and though it is not true in Christian doctrine (where the Trinity is the Father, the Son, and the Holy Spirit) it can be true in Christian devotion, as in Górecki's songs.[18] I find "God sensible to the heart" in the thought of "God with us," seeing my life as a journey in time and God as my companion on the way. I find myself longing, nevertheless, for human companionship, visible and tangible, and when it is taken away, in the ebb tide of a human relationship, God's presence is night to my senses.

A divine presence is night to my senses, that is, when I am longing and looking in the direction of human companionship. When I look instead in the direction of the mystery, the night becomes luminous. I feel a kind of peacefulness when I say to myself, "My life is a journey in time, and God is my companion on the way," and even when I add, "I sometimes wish I had a human companion, visible and tangible." I feel a kind of peaceful wholeness, recognizing my feelings in conjunction with a peaceful vision of my whole life. In fact, I feel both a sense of serenity and a sense of adventure as I say "My life is a journey in time, and God is my companion on the way." When I add that other thought, "I sometimes wish I had a human companion, visible and tangible," I am letting my vision illumine the night of my senses. I am letting the peaceful night illumine the restless night, as Barthes says quoting Saint John of the Cross, "And the night was dark and it illuminated the night."[19]

I think of *Transfigured Night*, the music by Arnold Schoenberg based on a poem by Richard Dehmel, where the night becomes luminous with the love of a man and a woman.[20] Here in the poem "Dark Night" by Saint John of the Cross the night becomes luminous with the love of God. If we love with a love we do not know, and if the love we do not know is really the love of God, then the peaceful vision of the love of God, "My life is a journey in time, and God is my companion on the way," is capable of illumining the restless night of human longing, "I sometimes wish I had a human companion, visible and tangible." How? I may find freedom, as in the story of a man who has fallen in love with a mermaid:

> "What if I offer you freedom?"
> "Freedom?"
> "From her."
> "No."[21]

And even though I refuse it like this, I may eventually become heart-free just contemplating the vision of a journey with God in time. And then again if I am willing to walk with God, if I am willing to let be and be open to the mystery, I may find human companionship on my way after all—"you may find friends on your way when you least look for it."[22]

One who loves God, according to Spinoza, is one who takes pleasure in the idea of God, one who "rejoices with the idea of God."[23] That is what I find myself doing, rejoicing with the idea of my life as a journey in time and God as my companion on the way. Can the love of God be as simple as this? I recall seeing a (Czech?) film about a man who had a nervous breakdown and afterwards could not sustain a human relationship. At first he could relate only to a dog, then later to a child, the girl to whom the dog had belonged. Only at the very end of the film does he begin to relate again to an adult, a woman who had been his friend before his breakdown. Is the love of God as simple as the love of an animal? Or is it like the love of a child? Or is it like the love of an adult? "One who understands oneself and one's emotions clearly and distinctly loves God," Spinoza says, "and the more so the more one understands oneself and one's emotions."[24] So if I understand my own love of an animal, my own love of a child, my own love of an adult clearly and distinctly, I love God, and the more I understand the loves of my life the more I love God.

Understanding myself and my emotions in the ebb tide of a human relationship is thus my way of loving God in my "night of sense." It means being patient with myself and my emotions. It means waiting on God without knowing what to expect. Will the ebb tide be followed by the flood tide of the human relationship? Will I simply become heart-free? Will I find new friendship where I least look for it? All I know is that by abiding in the love of God I will come to wisdom rather than to bitterness and resentment. Although I cannot simply will away my emotions, I am free to choose how I will relate to them. Wisdom means relating to them with understanding. Bitterness and resentment come of a refusal to understand. I suppose the essential thing is simply to choose wisdom, as Solomon did when God said "Ask what I shall give you," to choose "an understanding mind."[25]

What then do I come to understand? My "night of sense" has to do largely with human love and friendship, I can see, but as I come to understand it better I can see it has to do with the love of God, and the love of God, I can see too, is not simply an emotion among others but is the conscious direction of my life as a journey with God in time. I can understand the hurt I feel in the ebb tide of a human relationship, but at the same time I understand I have to let go of the hurt, and indeed am free to let go of it in the vision of my life as a journey with God. I mention Spinoza here because, as Novalis says of him, he was "a man inebriated with God,"[26] and that is where I have to go to be heart-free, towards being caught up ever more consciously in love's direction. It is true, the experience of being caught up in the love of God, as I know it, is an experience of peace, of living in the peace of the present, in the peace of the Presence. I find peace like this just reading things that restore my perspective when I have been upset, e.g., reading Tolkien even though there is no mention of God there, I find the sense of a journey in time in which I am "guided and guarded."

That sense of being "guided and guarded,"[27] Tolkien's phrase, is my sense of God as my companion on the journey of life. It is the way I know "God sensible to the heart." Although I have mentioned Spinoza here on the love of God, I realize his concept of God is very different from mine, much more impersonal than mine. Still, the influence of God, according to Spinoza, is pervasive. What is more, God's influence is intelligent, not mindless. (Here I am arguing like Spinoza.) It is this pervasive and intelligent influence I am speaking of when I use Tolkien's phrase "guided and guarded." I am taking God's pervasive and intelligent influence as a kind of companionship.

As I understand it, different notions of God reflect different relationships with God, a personal God a personal relationship, an impersonal God an impersonal relationship. Union with God for Spinoza means being caught up in the love of God for God but not seeking a return of love from God. Being caught up in the love of God, for me, means being known and loved, and union with God for me means knowing and being known, loving and being loved. It is one and the same God, as I understand it, but Spinoza's relationship is one purely and simply of knowing and loving, mine is one also of being known and being loved. For me the sense of being led by God, of being "guided and guarded," is a sense of being known and being loved. It is true, this experience is night to my senses, it can seem a lot of nothing to my senses, but if I open my heart it becomes "God sensible to the heart." It means taking the little light I have in my life and letting it guide me and guard me. It means seeing the inner light with my heart when all my eyes see is darkness.

"To darken this darkness, this is the gate of all wonder,"[28] Barthes concludes, quoting Lao-tzu. If I choose "an understanding mind," if I choose wisdom, I am darkening the darkness of my senses, as it were, letting go of the fulfilment of my senses, letting go of bitterness and resentment at the unfulfilment of my senses, but I am opening the gate to an integration of sense and spirit. For to choose wisdom is to abandon myself to the will of God, like the people who say *Dios lo quiere.* It is to become like the people who "can't hold on to sadness." I come like them to a happiness, a well-being of sense and spirit. I come to a wholeness that is a healing of the hurt I have taken in the ebbing of friendship. I come to a letting go, a letting be that feels like well-being, like joy. My "night of sense" becomes "a lucky night," "a happy night" (*una noche dichosa*).

Integration of sense and spirit comes of being caught up in the love of God, it seems, of loving with "all your heart, and with all your soul, and with all your might." I can see an integration of sense and spirit in the prologues of John, "And the Word was made flesh, and dwelt among us, and we beheld his glory . . ." in the prologue of the Gospel, and "That which was from the beginning, which we have heard, which we have seen with our eyes, which we have looked upon, and our hands have handled, of the Word of life" in the prologue of the Epistle.[29] Perhaps this letting be that I have been talking about, this letting go of the fulfilment of my senses, this letting go of bitterness and resentment at their unfulfilment, opens the gate to the wonder of incarnation, to the unity of sense and spirit in incarnation. To choose wisdom, to choose "an understanding mind," can be to choose this Word of life, this Word that became flesh and dwelt among us, to go from "In the beginning was the Word" to something like "In the end is the Word," like Broch's Virgil who comes in the end to realize "it was the word beyond speech."

To come to "the word beyond speech," however, it seems I must pass like Broch's Virgil through a "night of spirit." As I am interpreting it here, a "night of sense" is a dark night of love passing through loneliness, and a "night of spirit" is that same dark night when it becomes a night of loneliness in the face of death. "And if you should lose each other," the Lady of Wisdom says in *The Golden Key*, "do not be afraid, but go on and on."[30] For if we go through this night like Broch's Virgil, letting go of everyone and everything only to come into a new relationship with everyone and everything, then this night too can become "a happy night."

The Night of Spirit

I may enter a kind of night of spirit when my life opens up before me all the way to death. If I perceive the lack of perception in my work, in my words and music, I may become like Broch's Virgil on his deathbed, ready to burn his lifework. For I perceive "the cloud of unknowing" that comes between me and God, the cloud that can be pierced only by love:

> Love shines through the cloud which came between the Lover and the Beloved, and made it as bright and resplendent as is the moon by night, as the day-star at dawn, the sun at midday, the understanding in the will; and through that bright cloud the Lover and the Beloved held converse.[31]

Here I am quoting not *The Cloud of Unknowing* but Ramon Lull. But it is this "converse," it is God's communing with the soul that is night to the soul according to Saint John of the Cross. It is the very perception I perceive lacking in my work, a perception that comes to me as love rather than knowledge, love shining through the darkness of my unknowing.

When I read Saint John of the Cross on "the night of spirit," I feel the inadequacy of my own experience in trying to understand his, even more than when I read him on "the night of sense." I am coming out of an experience of heart's longing, but he is coming out of an experience of pure love of God. Passing over to him and his experience, I find many resonances in myself. Left to myself in the ebb tide of a human relationship, I look to God and to the presence of God, finding peace in the thought of my life as a journey with God in time. Left to himself in the ebb tide of a relationship with God, the saint also looks to God, but more desperately than I, for his night is darker, deprived of the luminous presence of God. The saint is like Christ crying out, "My God, my God, why have you forsaken me?" All the saint experiences is the "ray of divine darkness"[32] that the mystics speak of, as if it were an infrared light or an ultraviolet light, a ray of love that passes through the cloud of our unknowing, the presence of God indeed but a dark presence, a presence that is darkness not only to our senses but even to our spirit in its longing for understanding.

Well, I do have that longing for understanding, the heart's longing to know and be known, to love and be loved, the longing for a knowing that is loving, a loving that is knowing. I seem to know also what Broch's Virgil means when he says,

> The converse with the inscrutable! Oh, as long as the invisible cloudy cover stretched between above and below was not pierced, the prayer brought back only its own echo; the god remained unreachable, he vouchsafed no answer.[33]

It is love that pierces the cloudy cover, the longing that becomes the love, and the longing itself is "from God and of God and towards God." It is true, the longing comes from this side, not the other side of the cloudy cover, but God is on this side, I want to say, as well as the other side.

Maybe then I can understand the night of pure love from the night of longing that I know. Let me see if I can follow longing as it becomes love and pierces the cloud of unknowing between us and God. No doubt it is possible if the heart's longing really is the love of God in us and it is all a matter of "realizing" something that is already real.

As long as I am looking for love to come to me from the outside, I live in unrequited longing. It is when I realize the heart's longing is the love of God in me that I realize God is with me, I am caught up in the love of God, I am in love with God. But then, if it is already in me, it seems the love of God is subtle and pervasive. It is not what I expected. I have to "walk in dark and pure faith," as Saint John of the Cross says quoting the prophet, "I will betroth thee—that is, I will unite thee—with me through faith."[34] I do feel I am walking "in dark and pure faith" when I am walking with God "with no light or guide," as in the poem, "other than that burning in my heart." There is indeed the experience of the heart's longing, the light "burning in my heart," but it is "dark and pure faith" to take the heart's longing as the love of God within me. I have to believe in the love of God, to believe I am loved, to believe I love, when it seems to me, as to Broch's Virgil, "love is the reality" I am still seeking and what I "had held to be love had been only yearning."

When the old Bedouin in the desert said "The love is from God and of God and towards God," T. E. Lawrence was filled with wonder. "I had believed Semites unable to use love as a link between themselves and God," Lawrence said, "indeed, unable to conceive such relation except with the intellectuality of Spinoza, who loved so rationally and sexlessly, and transcendentally that he did not seek, or rather had not permitted, a return."[35] Here I am now trying to use the heart's longing as a link between myself and God, taking the heart's longing to be that very love that is "from God and of God and towards God," seeing love and its return in the "from and of and towards" of the heart's longing. The love, according to this, is first of all "from God," and so the return is not of God to us but of us to God, "towards God." Meanwhile the love is "of God," is God's love in us, and so is not a matter of achieving but of recognizing love.

I am in a story of recognition, therefore, a story in which I come to recognize the love of God. A moment of recognition comes for me whenever my life opens up before me all the way to death. I meet myself at the horizon, as Heidegger says, and the self I meet is my eternal self, myself in love with God. When I become vividly aware that I will die someday, I mean, I realize the only thing that matters in my life is the love of God. To be sure, realizing it is the only thing that matters is one thing; realizing I am in love with God is another. I have to merge with my eternal self, it seems, to realize I am in love with God. That is what seems to happen in the last part of Broch's *Death of Virgil*. There Broch writes in capital letters:

> THEREUPON HE WAS PERMITTED TO TURN AROUND;
> THEREUPON CAME THE COMMAND TO TURN AROUND;
> AND THEREUPON HE WAS TURNED AROUND.[36]

When I enter into my eternal self, I am permitted to turn around, I am commanded to turn around, I am turned around. I am looking in the direction I have not been looking. I am looking in love's direction.

But what is the direction I was looking before I turned in love's direction? "The destination was unknown, unknown the harbor of departure; one was shoved off from no pier, coming out of infinity, pressing on to infinity," Broch says, "the journey went on of itself, nevertheless strict and true to its course, guided by a sure hand, and had it been permitted to turn around, one must have glimpsed the steersman at the helm, the helper in the unchartered, the pilot who was acquainted with the exit to the harbor."[37] Yes, that seems to describe my experience very well, a sense of being on a journey from the unknown into the unknown, a sense nevertheless of being guided and guarded. It is the experience of the heart's longing, of its direction "from and of and towards" the unknown. It is the sense of being on a journey with God in time.

So if I am permitted to turn around, if I am commanded to turn around, if I am turned around, I turn from the direction of my heart's restless movement to that of its repose. "Our heart is restless until it rests in you." I turn from time's arrow to love's direction. I think of love's direction as a transformation of time's arrow, the journey from the unknown into the unknown becoming a journey from God and to God. Broch images it as a turning around. The two images come together in that of meeting oneself at the horizon: I follow time's arrow to the horizon and then I turn around and see my journey in a new light as "from God and of God and towards God." Using the term Dasein, "being there," to describe human existence, Heidegger asks "What is it to have one's own death?" and answers "It is Dasein's running ahead to its past, to an extreme possibility of itself that stands before it in certainty and utter indeterminacy."[38] It is life's running ahead to death, that is, where life is past. And he goes on to say "This running ahead is nothing other than the authentic and singular future of one's own Dasein."[39] This running ahead to the point where life is past is itself the real future.

Running ahead, if I understand it rightly, is what I am doing here, running ahead to myself at the horizon, not actually dying but having my life open up before me all the way to death. "Dasein as human life is primarily being possible,"[40] Heidegger says. Being possible for me is being in love with God. It is for me the way of possibility. To love with all my heart, and with all my soul, and with all my might is to be whole, is my whole being. Here again, I am realizing love is all that counts in the face of death, love of God. I am realizing it is my way. But that is realizing only that it is my possibility, not that it is my actuality. Still, if human life is primarily being possible, I am indeed realizing the love of God.

If now I turn around and view my actual life in retrospect in the light of my possibility, I can see something more. Time is "the possible horizon for any understanding whatsoever of Being" in Heidegger's early thinking, but in his later thinking, after his "turn around" (*Kehre*), time is "the lighting up of the self-concealing" (*Lichtung des Sichverbergens*), the showing of the mystery that "shows itself and at the same time withdraws."[41] If I turn around and view my life in these terms, looking for the mystery, I find the love of God showing and withdrawing in my life. It is the mystery of my life. The love of God shows itself and conceals itself in my heart's longing. When my heart is kindled with hope, and my mind is illumined with vision, and I feel an inner peace, seeing my life as a journey in time and God as my companion on the way, then the mystery is showing itself. When the kindling dies down, and the vision fades, and I feel restless again, then the mystery is concealing itself.

A new vision is what Broch's Virgil comes to when he turns around or is turned around, a vision in which the universe does take on the coherence it used to have for him but in which he now sees something more, ultimately "it was the word beyond speech." For me the journey with God in time is the coherence life used to have for me. I come back to it when I turn around and view my life in retrospect, but do I come to something new to me? Yes, I believe I do, I come to see the love of God is the mystery of my life. Although Lawrence says he "loved so rationally and sexlessly, and transcendentally," I see rather a profound insight into human emotion in Spinoza that seems inseparable from his love of God, and I can hope for something like that myself if I take the love of God to be the mystery of my life.

"One always learns one's mystery at the price of one's innocence,"[42] Robertson Davies says, and that seems true for me here. Learning that the love of God is the mystery of my life, I can no longer be innocent in trying to find someone or something to fulfil my heart's longing. Still, the mystery not only "shows itself" but also "withdraws," and when it does withdraw, and the kindling of the love of God dies down, and the vision of the journey with God fades, and I feel restless again, I do long to find someone or something to fill up my emptiness. This then is my night of longing and my night of love. For I begin to doubt my love and my capacity for love. Broch's Virgil, turned around, sees a human visage in the universe, the image of the mother and the child, "the image of the boy in the arms of the mother, united to her in a sorrowful smiling love."[43] That is the image that pervades also Górecki's "Symphony of Sorrowful Songs." When I listen to the music, I can feel the power of the love, the love of the mother and the child, and I ask myself "What do I know of love?"

Yet then I remember that the heart's longing becomes the love, and that I do know the heart's longing, and I realize that is what enables me to feel the love in the music. That is the effect of music, according to E. M. Forster, "the passion of your life becomes more vivid."[44] I think of a song I have composed myself called "Rainbow Song":

> In the end is the Word
> as in the beginning,
> for we saw only a fog bow,
> just a moonbow,
> a white rainbow,
> but now we see inner light,
> and we are on a winding stair
> inside the rainbow,
> and all hues of being
> climb along with us,
> and we ascend we know
> into a land of heart's desire,
> for we can hear the music
> of a word beyond all speech.[45]

I am echoing Broch's *Death of Virgil* here, "it was the word beyond speech" (for him too the image of the rainbow is pervasive), as well as the Gospel of John, "In the beginning was the Word." I am reaching, though, toward a love that is "from God and of God and towards God," trying to understand the love from the heart's longing that I know.

It is the heart's longing that Broch himself seems to be describing in a very short paragraph just after saying "the images sank down," the images of mother and child, and just before the very long and final paragraph of his novel ending "it was the word beyond speech":

> The welling fountain of the middle, gleaming invisibly in the infinite anguish of knowing: the no thing filled the emptiness and it became the universe.[46]

Somehow there is a correspondence between the heart's longing and the word at the end. The heart's longing is a "welling fountain," "gleaming invisibly in the infinite anguish of knowing." It is a longing that is an unknowing love, that seems to suffer "infinite anguish" in coming to know itself or to know what it longs for, an emptiness that is a "no thing," the felt emptiness of desire that is our key to understanding "the emptiness" filled by the universe and named by "the word beyond speech." Passing through "the infinite anguish of knowing" is my "night of spirit," coming to know the love of God is the mystery of my life, and coming to know the mystery's showing and withdrawing.

There is indeed an "infinite anguish of knowing" in coming to know the love we do not know. Maybe that is what Spinoza is touching on when he says "One who loves God cannot strive that God should love one back," for he also says "the love of God for human beings and the mind's intellectual love of God is one and the same."[47] It is not that God does not love me, he is saying, but my love of God and God's love of me are one. I would say myself the love of God in us is *felt* as our heart's longing. There is "infinite anguish" in knowing this because I wanted my heart's longing to be fulfilled. But when I realize the love of God in me is felt as my heart's longing, that God draws me and I am drawn to God by my heart, I really do have to find rest in restlessness! I have to find rest in the very elusiveness of the mystery!

"How far it is from the knowledge of God to the love of God!"[48] Pascal exclaims. It is as far as from knowing the elusiveness of the mystery to following the mystery as it shows itself and again withdraws. That showing and withdrawing is a kind of leading, leading us on. *To love God is to follow the mystery, to be led by its showing and withdrawing.* That is love's direction! And that is how I can find rest in the elusiveness of the mystery! I see the showing and withdrawing in words and in music and in spiritual friendship, and so for

me there is a way of words and a way of music and a way of
spiritual friendship. When I encounter the withdrawing,
though, each of these ways seems to fail or dead-end. It is at
this point that I have to remember "love is a direction" and
to wait on the mystery to show itself again. I maintain the
direction in my waiting. Still, I am not waiting in vain, for
the mystery does show itself again and the way of words and
of music and of spiritual friendship opens up again before
me and proves to be a road like Tolkien's that "goes ever on
and on."

Waiting on God is the form love of God takes in these
times of withdrawal. I am waiting for my heart to speak, not
knowing what my heart is going to say, and yet believing
God will lead me by the heart. When my heart does speak,
"My heart speaks clearly at last,"[49] then love of God takes the
form of following the heart. If I think of the love as coming
from God and going to God, felt in me as my heart's longing, I am waiting for the love to kindle in my heart and to
illumine my path before me. Sometimes, though, I find
myself waiting not simply for my heart to speak clearly but
waiting for something to happen, for the situation I am in to
change. Is this waiting on God?

When the mystery shows itself, then something is happening, it is true, and that goes with a kindling of the heart.
The mystery shows itself in words when words speak to the
heart, in music when "the passion of your life becomes more
vivid," in friendship when "heart speaks to heart." It could be
essential, though, for me to be waiting simply on God and
not on one or another outcome, say for the flood tide when
I am in the ebb tide of a friendship. "It makes little difference whether a bird is tied by a thin thread or by a cord,"
Saint John of the Cross says. "For even if tied by thread, the
bird will be prevented from taking off just as surely as if it

were tied by cord."[50] I may be in the ebb tide of a friendship just for this purpose, to break the thread of my attachment to the friendship, to become heart-free and heart-whole in love with God. On the other hand, just when I have become willing to walk alone, I may find I have human companionship after all, like Frodo in Tolkien's story just when he has summoned up his courage to go alone, "It is no good trying to escape you. But I'm glad, Sam. I cannot tell you how glad. Come along! It is plain that we were meant to go together."[51]

I come then to "God sensible to the heart" in heartache and also in heartsease. If "the heart has its reasons that reason does not know,"[52] as Pascal says, these reasons can nevertheless become known to the mind, and that is what *insight* is. The mystery of a life is in these reasons that reason does not know, but the showing of the mystery is in their becoming known to the mind, my realizing for instance that the love of God is the mystery of my life. The withdrawing is in their being hidden from the mind. What I long for in these times of withdrawal, when I myself do not understand, is an understanding heart. I look to others; I look to God. Meanwhile I wait for insight, I wait for the heart's reasons to become known to my own mind. Moreover, I choose wisdom, I choose "an understanding mind" like Solomon, even before I have it.

If insight is what happens when reasons of the heart become known to the mind, then coming to insight is like remembering. It does feel like remembering, coming to know with my mind what I already know with my heart. It seems we always knew what we come to know and, as Plato says, "all enquiry and all learning is but recollection."[53] As I say this, though, I am thinking not so much of the pre-existence of the soul that Plato speaks of in the dialogue *Meno* as of the reasons of the heart. The mystery of a human life is there in the unknown reasons of the heart, and the mystery shows itself when they become known, as if we were remembering, and it conceals itself when they are hidden, as if we were forgetting. There are times when we "lose perspective," as if forgetting, and times when we "regain perspective," as if remembering. If time is "the lighting up of the self-concealing," that is because it is "a changing image of eternity." The reasons of the heart are eternal reasons, and the love of God is the mystery of our lives.

The Heart of Mystery

*And now Tangle felt that there was something
in her knowledge which was not yet in her
understanding . . . and the longer she looked the more
an indescribable vague intelligence went on rousing
itself in her mind.*

—George MacDonald[1]

Once I stood at a crossroads in life where the way of words
and the way of music diverged, and I chose the way of words.
Now I have come to a meeting of the ways where music has
rejoined words in my life. I have come to realize too that this
reunion in my own life echoes distantly some larger and
original unity words and music once had, for instance for
Saint Augustine writing *On Music*. I think also of spiritual
friendship, as related somehow to words and music, as belonging with them to what Shakespeare calls "the marriage
of true minds."[2] If spiritual friendship is the communion of
true minds, words and music are the communication of true
minds. I find myself seeking "the marriage of true minds" as
if it were my goal in life.

This unity I am seeking, of words and music and spiritual
friendship, is like the unity Heidegger was seeking of poetry
and thought, of thinking and thanking:

In the forest clearing to which his circular paths lead, though they do not reach it, Heidegger has postulated the unity of thought and poetry, of thought, of poetry, and of the highest act of mortal pride and celebration which is to give thanks.[3]

"Thinking is thinking" (*Denken ist Danken*),[4] a saying of seventeenth-century mystics, is Heidegger's watchword in this, and he sees thanking as the essence of poetry. For me thinking and thanking find expression not only in words but also in music. Indeed "we can know more than we can tell" and what we cannot tell in words we may yet express in music, and "the marriage of true minds" in spiritual friendship is a communing not only in what we can know and tell but also in what we can know and cannot tell. Still, there is also what we do not know. The element of the unknown in life, however, the mystery, "shows itself and at the same time withdraws," I find, in words and music and spiritual friendship. It shows itself in the flow and withdraws in the ebb of hope and peace and friendship and understanding.

"There are meaner metaphors to live by,"[5] George Steiner concludes of Heidegger's unity of poetry and thought, of thinking and thanking. I could say the same of the unity I am seeking—it is an ennobling metaphor of life. For to live in the unity of words and music would be to live in a thinking and thanking like that of Saint Augustine echoing Psalms with the story of his life. To live also in spiritual friendship would be to live like him and his friends pursuing wisdom in retirement from the world. When I am in the ebb tide of hope and peace and friendship and understanding, however, I find I have to live in the elusiveness of the mystery, letting it lead me hide-and-seek on a journey in time, as in Newman's song "Lead, Kindly Light." For me the unity of words and music and spiritual friendship is that of the mystery showing itself and withdrawing in human communion and communication. So it is the adventure with God, elusive and mysterious, the journey with God in time, that we sing in words and music, that we share in spiritual friendship.

What is more, if the mystery "shows itself and at the same time withdraws" in words and music and spiritual friendship, its presence is nevertheless abiding, even in the ebb tide of hope and peace and friendship and understanding. When I am feeling my loneliness, when I am feeling the lack of communion and communication, the thought of the journey with God in time seems to restore my perspective. It is as if God were saying "I am with you."

What is the mystery? My way of seeking "the marriage of true minds" has been that of "passing over," as I have called it, passing over from my own life to that of others and coming back again with new insight to my own. Passing over has been for me a way of words and also a way of spiritual friendship. It has become for me now a way of music too, as "we can know more than we can tell" and can express that "more" in music. For passing over to the words of another means entering into the tacit dimension of words, the very dimension that reaches expression in music. Passing over and coming back seem to correspond to the ebb and flow of human communion and communication, passing over to the flow and coming back to the ebb. When I am in the high tide of communion and communication I can pass over to others, but when I am in the low tide I have to come back again to myself and my aloneness. I have to be willing to walk alone while retaining my hope of communion and communication, and in my willingness and hope there is a sense of presence, of God with me, of "God sensible to the heart."

I find the music of time in the ebb and flow of inner life, in the passing over and coming back of human communion and communication. Once when I was visiting the Trappist Abbey of Gethsemane, I was speaking with Dom Timothy, the abbot, about monastic life, and I said I admired the life of the monks but I needed myself a lot of interaction with people. "Yes," he replied, "if you are very inward, you need a lot of interaction with people." Now, as I reflect on his words, I see I am very inward and in seeking "the marriage of true minds" I am seeking the interaction with people that will balance my inwardness. I can see the music of time, however, is present already in my inwardness, in the ebb and flow of inner life, before ever I come to the passing over and coming back of human communion and communication.

Reading Saint Augustine *On Music*, I find he relates the music of time to that of eternity with the thought of time as "a changing image of eternity." I addressed a song to him on this:

> Tell me, Master,
> how you turn
> from changing to unchanging number
> and are sensible to
> music of eternal life,
> or tell me rather how to listen
> to unchanging number in the changing
> and to hear eternal music
> in the song of earth.[6]

It is the eternal that "shows itself and at the same time withdraws" in time, showing itself in the flow of inner life and in the passing over of communion and communication and withdrawing in the ebb and in the coming back to oneself. Time is there in the ebb and flow, and eternity is there in "the singing timelessness of the heart,"[7] as Broch calls it in *The Death of Virgil*. Or in Saint Augustine's own terms, time is there in the restless movement of the heart, and eternity is there in the repose of the heart in God.

There is restless movement in words and music and spiritual friendship, and there is also rest. If reading is "that fruitful miracle of a communication in solitude,"[8] as Proust says in his essay *On Reading*, there is a peaceful rest in the restless to-and-fro of passing over to the other and coming back to oneself, and if reading can turn into singing, as he imagines at the end of the essay, envisioning a reader of the Gospel of Luke beginning to chant the Canticle of Mary or the Canticle of Zachary, there can be a peaceful rest in the restless movement also of music. I think of Arvo Pärt's *Magnificat*,[9] where there is a sense of repose, almost of stasis, in all the movement of words and music, and I think of Pärt's dedicatory quotation at the beginning of a composition in memory of the film director Andre Tarkovsky, "The temple bell stops, but the sound keeps coming from the flowers."[10] There is a sense in that dedication of lasting words, of lasting music, and of lasting friendship.

A lasting love is one that is alive in memory. It is true, a life can take the course of an increasing aloneness, like the lives of animals, for instance whales who go in herds when they are younger but go alone when they are older like Moby Dick.[11] A human life can end "alone with the Alone" in deep solitude, but it can lead also to being alone with the human alone in deep communion. As I recollect the loves of my life, my love of words, of music, of spiritual friendship, I find that longing "to know that we are not alone." Seeking "the marriage of true minds," I find not so much that we are unalone as that we can be alone with the human alone in communion and communication and with the divine Alone in a union of love. If life does take the course of an increasing aloneness, there are deserted places of the heart in memory, "deserted cities of the heart"[12] like the abandoned cities of the Yucatan.

If I am learning to be alone with the alone, with the human as well as the divine alone, these deserted places are like the divine desert of Meister Eckhart where I find the silence of words, the silence of music, the silence of friendship. There is the silence that is broken when words begin and the silence that ensues when words end. It is as if all the stories I remember, going back to childhood, were all one story that begins and ends in silence and so tells of everything coming from the silence and returning to the silence, like the Word in the Gospel of John that comes from God and returns to God. And it is as if all the names of things I learned from childhood on were syllables of this one Word that comes out of silence and returns into silence, as if "My name and yours, and the true name of the sun, or a spring of water, or an unborn child, all are syllables of the great word that is very slowly spoken by the shining of the stars."[13]

Silence here is silence as in "We all have within us a center of stillness surrounded by silence." I take this surrounding silence to be the presence of God and that center of stillness to be our deep self, the center where the circles of words and music and spiritual friendship intersect. Music also breaks the silence and ends in silence, though "The temple bell stops, but the sound keeps coming from the flowers." Music breaks a silence that is still there when words are being spoken. It is the silence of the untold, what is untold in the telling of the story. Friendship too, when it is spiritual friendship, a communion of the alone with the human alone, breaks the silence of communion with the divine Alone, the silence of the presence of God, only to share the presence with another human being, to meet where we are most alone. I see then friendship in its ebb tide returning into the silence. Perhaps that is how I may understand that ebb, that withdrawal I find so hard to accept.

"It lies in the nature of every finally perfect love that sooner or later it may no longer reach the loved one save in the infinite,"[14] Rilke says in a letter. Reaching the loved one in the infinite, it seems, is reaching the loved one in the silence into which words and music and friendship return. It means living in this peaceful vision of everything coming out of the divine silence and returning into the divine silence. Alone with the alone, human and divine, is really all one. It is like Plotinus's vision of everything coming from the One and returning to the One, his vision of the dance of everyone and everything around God. "And we are always around it (the One) but do not always look at it," he says; "it is like a choral dance . . . but when we do look to him (God), then we are at our goal and at rest and do not sing out of tune as we dance our god-inspired dance around him."[15]

For me the vision changes into one of a journey with God in time, for our center of stillness surrounded by silence is a moving center like the eye of a hurricane moving along a path in time. To stay in the center I have to keep moving or I will be caught in the outer edges of storm and destruction. Still, what Plotinus says about looking to God is true, I am not always looking to God but when I do look to God I am at my goal and am at rest even in the restless movement of the dance, of the journey. There is, moreover, a sense of adventure, of hope, in my movement along a path in time, balancing the serenity of circling around the center. When I am dismayed, I find myself returning to this vision of a journey with God in time, reading Tolkien for instance for his sense of a road that "goes ever on and on" into the unknown. "There are also times in life," as Jean Giono once said, "when a person has to rush off in pursuit of hopefulness."[16]

Rushing off in pursuit of hopefulness can mean letting go of something I have set my heart upon and opening my heart again to the hopefulness of the journey with God in time, "and you may find friends upon your way when you least look for it."[17] There is hope of "the marriage of true minds," I tell myself as I throw myself once again into the journey with God. "Where is the dancing? Where is the way?" I ask myself as I look for the direction of hope and hopefulness, "Story is our only boat for sailing on the river of time, but in the great rapids and the winding shallows, no boat is safe."[18] My story of a journey with God in time can carry me through the great rapids of longing and the winding shallows of loneliness, I believe, as long as I stay in it and do not succumb to phantoms of fear and sadness.

"Keep me friendly to myself, keep me gentle in disappointment"[19] is a prayer that makes sense if I am living not simply in irreversible time but with the Eternal in time. The presence of the Eternal means time is not irreparable. I can be friendly to myself, I can be gentle in disappointment, if I can believe I am on a journey with God, if I can believe God is my companion on the way, if I can believe God is with me. For if my life is a journey in time and God is by my side, then it is very different than if God were simply my goal far ahead, and I were here far away from God. Instead the goal is with me, "we are at our goal and at rest and do not sing out of tune as we dance our god-inspired dance around him," and disappointment is nothing up against the presence of all good at my side. My relationship to myself, that is, and my relationship to my life and to what happens to me is based on my relationship with God. If God is with me, then I can be with myself.

Time is the flow of longing, and if I let the longing in my loneliness become prayer, I begin to *realize* the journey with God in time. I mean it becomes more than a vision of life, it becomes a real adventure. I begin to feel the presence of God, the timeless presence in time, and I begin to realize the longing is the love of God in me. The prayer can be without words, like a song without words, or it can be with words, like

> Lead kindly Light,
> amid the encircling gloom . . .

As my longing becomes prayer, as it becomes conscious, willing, hopeful, I become like Giono's "man who planted hope and grew happiness."[20]

What hope do I have? "Attention is the natural prayer of the soul," especially attention, as Paul Celan says, to "the mystery of encounter."[21] There is mystery in our encounter with each other because of our emergence and separation from one another. If there is an original union from which we come and a final reunion to which we go, the longing in our loneliness will look for that original union, that final re-union in our encounter, however emerged and separated we have become. My longing, grown attentive in prayer, will find hints of union and reunion in my encounter with others, hints, elusive hints, a mystery that "shows itself and at the same time withdraws." That union we have left behind, that reunion that is still to come, I will sense in my encounter with others, as I let the longing in my loneliness become attention, as I let it become prayer. "They still love you," I may hope as I look backward, even after I have become separated from my friends, "and you may find friends upon your way when you least look for it," I may hope as I look forward, even before I have actually found the road of reunion in love.

I find hope in Grimm's words, "But one human heart goes out to another, undeterred by what lies between." If I am separated from the ones I love, my heart goes out to them, and if I am separated from a friend, my heart goes out to my friend, and perhaps my friend's heart goes out to me, undeterred by our separation. That "perhaps," that uncertainty, is a source of pain, but there may be enough contact to know it is true, that the other's heart does indeed go out to me. At any rate, I can find hope in this in the midst of separation. Love is a going out of one human heart to another, a going out to the reality of the other, just as knowledge is a taking in of the reality of the other, a coming back to myself, and can be even a knowledge that I am loved.

"You see, the brooks and the flowers and the birds come together," Grimm writes, "but people do not." That is because of our emergence and separation from nature and from one another. Still, if "one human heart goes out to another, undeterred by what lies between," our emergence and separation do not take away our union and reunion. What is more, if it is compatible with our emergence and separation, our union and reunion is spiritual, is relational. The Word in the beginning expresses our union; the Word at the end expresses our reunion. Is a spiritual, a relational union or reunion enough for me? There are times when it is enough for me, when I am in my "center of stillness surrounded by silence," when I can feel the peace of my center of stillness, the presence of the surrounding silence. And there are times when it is not enough for me, when I can feel the "four perturbations of the mind," when I can feel desire for the presence of a friend, gladness at the thought of meeting again, fear of losing contact, sadness at our separation.

When I am feeling the love of God, when I am thinking of God with joy, as Spinoza says, then it seems a spiritual, a relational union or reunion is enough, and that union or re-union can be described as "I and thou." "So, waiting, I have won from you the end: God's presence in each element," Buber quotes from Goethe as the motto of his *I and Thou*, or "Thus I have finally obtained from you by waiting God's presence in all elements."[22] For the "I and thou" is a rela-tionship not only with God, not only with human beings, but even with trees, and God's presence, the "I and thou" with God, is there in that with human beings and with other living beings. As I understand it, we pass from "I and it" to "I and thou" by letting go of "it." Letting go of the object of our longing, of "it," we pass from longing to love, or we re-alize our heart's yearning is really the love of God in us.

But before letting go of "it," when I am yearning for ful-filment, when I am feeling a spiritual union or reunion is *not* enough for me, I can let my longing become prayer. I can encompass the "I and it" of my longing in the "I and thou" of prayer, letting my longing become prayer, and letting prayer become music. This is the way I come to letting go. That simple African love song,

> I walk alone,

is a perfect expression of the longing in my loneliness. Per-haps I can regard it as having the virtue of a prayer. I think of Simone Weil reciting George Herbert's poem "Love." "I

used to think I was merely reciting it as a beautiful poem,"
she says, "but without my knowing it the recitation had the
virtue of a prayer."[23] So it may be with my African love song,
it may be in effect a prayer, a simple prayer like "Help!" or
perhaps a more implicit prayer like the Psalm "Lover and
friend hast thou put far from me."[24]

Now if I let my song "I walk alone" become Jazz or Blues
or Soul or Country or Rock or Metal, if I let it become
music as a state of being, I am letting it become prayer as a
state of being. Like music, prayer can exist as a state of being
and it can exist as symbolic form. As a state of being, prayer
can be continuous, as the Russian pilgrim describes it in *The
Way of a Pilgrim*, going from Christ on his lips to Christ in
his thoughts to Christ in his heart.[25] If "I walk alone" becomes prayer, I go from walking alone to walking alone with
the Alone. As a state of being, therefore, it is no longer a
state of being alone but of being alone with the Alone and
thus really of being unalone. The answer to the prayer, or at
least an answer, is in the prayer itself.

Another answer is in "the mystery of encounter," in the
encounter with another human being, if my prayer becomes
"attention" to "the mystery of encounter." As symbolic
form, prayer can be the expression of all "the perturbations
of the mind," of desire and gladness, of fear and sadness. I
think of the Psalms. There is peace in prayer as symbolic
form with its beginning and middle and end, giving symbolic
form, beginning and middle and end, to the perturbations
themselves. As Saint Augustine echoes Psalms in his *Confessions*, or Stravinsky in his *Symphony of Psalms*, I can find
Psalms to express the desire and gladness, the fear and sadness in my loneliness. And I can become attentive to events
in the light of these feelings, or in the light of the peace I

come to in prayer. If I let my song "I walk alone" become a motet like the *Ave Verum*, my prayer becomes attention to "the mystery of encounter" in Christ where "alone with the Alone" becomes "all one." The answer to my prayer, I mean, becomes the presence of God among us, Emmanuel or "God with us." It is the same answer I find when "I walk alone" becomes prayer as a state of being, namely "I walk with God," but with a difference, "God walks with me" or rather "God walks with us."

Indeed if I become attentive to events in the light of my loneliness, grown peaceful now in prayer, I can find "the mystery of encounter" in my human relations. The inner peace of prayer casts my encounters with others in another light than that of raw loneliness. "Our relation to our fellow human beings is that of prayer," Kafka's saying, comes true for me, while the other half of it is still true, "our relation to ourselves" is "that of striving" and "from prayer we draw the strength for our striving." There is still a striving that comes of unrequited loneliness, and a drawing of strength from the inner peace of prayer that enables us to go on striving.

To go on then from striving to prayer in relation to ourselves, to come to live in the peace of prayer, that is "the road of the union of love with God." There is a "night of sense" and a "night of spirit" on this road insofar as my striving is for a fulfilment of sense and of spirit, and to pass from striving to prayer in relation to myself means letting go of fulfilment, the "it" in the "I and it" of longing, in order to live in the "I and thou" of love. Striving has really been essential to my relationship with myself. I have been living in the longing of my heart. My striving comes of the unrequited loneliness of my heart, and as long as my loneliness remains unrequited there is a darkness in my heart. "When the heart casts a shadow instead of dancing light, there story begins."[26]

A story begins for me at the point where my heart casts a shadow of loneliness and longing, for there I become vulnerable to "the mystery of encounter." I remember writing in a diary at the beginning of a long journey alone through South America, "My life is a journey in time, and God is my companion on the way," but I added "Sometimes I wish I had a human companion, visible and tangible." That addition was the shadow my heart was casting. "The poem is lonely," Celan says. "It is lonely and *en route*. Its author stays with it."[27] So it is also with the story. It is lonely and on a journey and I stay with it. All the same, there is "dancing light" for me in those first words, "My life is a journey in time, and God is my companion on the way."

Light and shadow are inseparable here, and my night of sense and spirit is in the shadow of loneliness and longing cast by my heart. Putting it this way, I can see there is a day as well as a night of sense, a day as well as a night of spirit. Daybreak comes when my heart casts dancing light instead of a shadow. Going through the night of sense and spirit means learning to love "with all your heart, and with all your soul, and with all your might." If the love of God is simply the idea of God accompanied by the feeling of joy, as Spinoza says, then the love of God is there when my heart casts dancing light, when I think with joy of my life as a journey with God in time. The love of God is easy! But it is one thing to love God and it is quite another thing to be caught up heart and soul in the love of God. That being caught up is what the night of sense and spirit seems to be about, coming to be caught up sense and spirit in the idea of God and in the feeling of joy. For me it means being caught up sense and spirit in the journey with God in time.

I am caught up in the journey with God when I am caught up in prayer as a state of being, and even when I am caught up in prayer as symbolic form and am giving expression to the journey with God in words and music. I think also of Tolkien's song cycle *The Road Goes Ever On*, where there is no explicit mention of God. When I am composing lyrics and music myself about the journey with God in time, I am caught up in it, sense and spirit. The dancing light is there but there is also the shadow of loneliness and longing. I haven't gotten rid of the shadow, but I have let it come to expression in my prayer, I have let it come to words and music. It is "emotion recollected in tranquillity," as Wordsworth says of poetry, desire and gladness, fear and sadness recollected in the peace of prayer.

Mystery shows itself in the light and at the same time withdraws in the shadow. It shows itself in the light of the journey with God in time and withdraws in the shadow of loneliness and longing. I walk alone and unalone. Perhaps that should be my song then,

I walk alone and unalone,

and it is a love song, but it hints of the love of God, and it seems to say human love is a shadow cast by the dancing light of the love of God. Still, the deeper shadow in human affairs is one of lovelessness, or of a longing and a loneliness that does not know itself as love. When I sing "I walk alone" as a love song, I already know my longing and my loneliness as love, human love. And when I sing "I walk alone and unalone," I know it as the love of God, and I know *the mystery is the love of God, and the mystery encompasses both the light of a journey and a joy and the shadow of a longing and a loneliness.*

"Gatekeepers don't leave the gate," the Gatekeeper says in Patricia McKillip's story. "But what my heart does, flying out of me in terror or wonder or love, only you can tell me, because it will follow only you."[28] Knowledge keeps the gate of the soul, taking in what it can of reality, but love goes out into reality, following God on a journey beyond all we know. There is discrimination in knowledge, letting some things in, keeping other things out, and there is also commitment in personal knowledge, a faithfulness that can lead to faith. But love becomes prayer, attention, letting God tell us our story, and what our heart does in prayer, flying out of us in terror or wonder or love, only God can tell us, because our heart will follow only God. To say "our heart will follow only you" is like saying "our heart is restless until it rests in you."

Attention, listening to God tell my story, is letting love lead to knowledge. My journey and my joy, my longing and my loneliness come together in a way I did not foresee. Paying attention to "the mystery of encounter," I find something of my journey and my joy that speaks to my longing and my loneliness. I begin to see my journey with God in time as a story of encounter, as Celan sees the poem. "The poem intends another, needs this other, needs an opposite. It goes toward it, bespeaks it," he says. "For the poem, everything and everybody is a figure of the other toward which it is heading."[29] So it is with the story of my journey with God in time. Everyone and everything I meet on the journey belongs to "the mystery of encounter," and so everyone and everything belongs to my journey and my joy, and everyone and everything speaks to my longing and my loneliness.

> In the ebb of love and friendship
> I can count upon the music of time
> to bring back again the flow,
> —I can hope we meet again,

a secret timeless place in my heart
coming back to life
and waiting on the slow dance of time
to reveal a path into the dawn,
for God is my companion on the way,
and I can live in inner peace
and follow inner light
of mystery that shows itself
in our encounter dark
and then withdraws into the light.

Lyric Theatre

Words and music have come together for me in lyric theatre while writing this book. I composed lyrics and music first for "The Church of the Poor Devil," using the story behind a book I had written some years ago with that title. There is a tiny chapel called the Church of the Poor Devil (Igreja do Pobre Diabo) at Manaus in Brazil, where the Rio Negro joins the Amazon. It is actually a chapel of Santo Antonio, patron of weddings. The action takes place there in the 1890s during the Rubber Boom. The soprano sings the part of Cordolina, who owns a bar and has just built the chapel. The tenor sings the part of Antonio, who owns a cabaret and lives with Cordolina but is afraid of marrying her and calls himself "the poor devil." The soprano also sings the part of Joana, who invokes the spirits for Antonio, and the tenor also sings the part of Santo Antonio, who answers Cordolina's prayers. A single dancer interprets the songs and does the Dance of the Spirits. We had a performance of the songs and dances (I left out the speaking parts) at Notre Dame in Pasquerilla East on November 23, 1993, with Karen Wonder as soprano, Patrick Birge as tenor, Lisa DeBoer as dancer, and myself at the piano.

After writing the chapter "This World's a City Full of Straying Streets," I composed lyrics and music for "The Golden Key," a story by George MacDonald, a fairy tale he wrote for children in the middle of the nineteenth century. The soprano sings the part of Tangle, a girl who becomes a woman in the story. The alto sings the part of the Great Aunt and then of the Lady in the Forest and then of the Wind Spirit. The tenor sings the part of Mossy, a boy who becomes a man in the story. And the baritone, who is also the narrator reading short selections of the story between songs and dances, sings the part of the Old Man of the Sea, the Old Man of the Earth, and the Ancient Child (= the Old Man of the Fire). A single dancer interprets the songs and does the Rainbow Dance, the Shadow Dance, the Circle Dance of Light, and the reprise of the Rainbow Dance at the end. We had a performance at Notre Dame in Pasquerilla East on April 4, 1995, with Brenda Wonder as soprano, Maura Pheney as alto, Jeffrey Graham as tenor, James Foster as baritone and narrator, Kathryn Turner as dancer, and myself at the piano.*

> *Steve Rossigno made a video recording of "The Church of the Poor Devil" at the actual performance on November 23, 1993, and of "The Golden Key" at the dress rehearsal on April 3, 1995.

THE CHURCH OF THE POOR DEVIL

Prelude

O Light (*Chorus*)
O light,
before me
and behind me,
on my right
and on my left!
O light
where are you
I am lost,
show me the way!
O light,
shine on
divided heart,
and wandering eye,
and my poor devil's cry!

Look, my chapel (*Cordolina*)
Look, my chapel,
all I've wanted to achieve
by work of light
and play of shadow,
helping prayer
to sound unsounding space
and echo silent time,
reshaping matter,
brick and stone and tile
    mosaic,
on the golden section

of the sun and moonlight,
all with one poor workman
carrying the sign of spirit
come what may!

The Poor Devil (*Antonio*)
Are you the devil?
No, the poor devil!
—I am called daimonic
for my will that is inspired,
that seeks the simple life
that is also intense,
and yet inclining to dispersal
as my willing falls asunder
and my mind is all imagining
from feeling over
and against my life.
Are you the devil?
No, the poor devil!

Eternal Vision (*Cordolina*)
Eternal vision
with you saints
we ask in faith
and confidence,
our candles shining
in the dark
that could not overcome
eternal light,
our voices bringing

hopes and fears
into the silence broken
by the Word
already spoken
of eternal life.

The Deadly Clear Path
(*Antonio*)
I fear the deadly clear path
into a future that is known,
a path across a daylight plain
to a horizon I can see;
I want instead to go by night
upon a path of the unknown
where I can never see the
    end,
where each turn is discovery,
and all my life is journeying
and is also serene in love,
for that is all
my heart's desire,
to live in hope
and joy in love.

All My Fears (*Cordolina*)
All my fears pursuing me,
all my regrets,
I bring before you here,
for you have access to the
    Only One
who knows the secrets of
    our hearts,

and I pray, promise to
    promise
to bring me inner light
to choose my path
into the unknown of my
    life,
but you always answer me
I am to go into my inner
    dark
with love instead of fear,
and take the unseen hand of
    God
for light instead of certainty.

Eternal Life (*Santo Antonio*)
Eternal life
belongs to us
when we live in the presence,
being inside God
as if God were a giant tree
alive and hollow all around
    us,
when we cast aside regret
    and fear
as if the fearful had already
    happened
and left nothing to regret,
for everyone and everything
    we lost
comes back again,
and every road we have not
    taken

joins the road of heart's
    desire
as it goes ever on and on.

A Woman Child (*Cordolina*)
When I was a woman child
I was all earth,
a square of earth, a dot of
    heaven,
and when I was growing,
heaven filled my earth,
a circle in my square.
and now grown-up I tend a
    bar,
earth fills my heaven,
but I build a chapel,
heaven closes round my
    earth,
my square inside my
circle,
and someday near death
I will be only heaven,
only circle with a dot of
    earth.

My Joy (*Santo Antonio*)
My joy is to be nothing,
to do nothing,
to think nothing,
but to let the universal
    life,
expressed as human,

flow in on me
and express itself again
through my acts and my
    thoughts
—I am not All,
I am not absorbed,
or I would not know I have
    nothing,
even my own body,
even my own claim to
    heaven,
but only this life in love.

I am mother (*Joana*)
I am mother of the saint
they tell in sorcery
while dancing, drumming,
    chanting
of my mothercraft,
for everyone and everything
    is here,
all earth and sky,
all spirits, all mortals too,
all the living and the dead,
for I am mother to these
    spirits,
and they are to me as
    children
and obey and disobey me
while I live, but I will die
someday and be myself
a child among the dead.

To Be Alone (*Antonio*)
It is not good
to be alone,
and yet I am afraid
to promise until death
—"O happy onliness!
O only happiness!"
the words I saw inscribed
upon a cloister wall
show us a way alone
a last a loved
along the riverrun of time,
but happy onliness?
and only happiness?
if it were not for love.

To Be a Saint (*Antonio* and
    Joana)
(*Antonio*) To be a saint
is to go past
a human happiness,
to love only
and to be loved,
to know only
and to be known.
(*Joana*) And not to be a saint
is misery the only misery,
if your call is
to live clear
down in your heart
and in your soul,
(*both*) to be a saint.

It is not too late (*Joana*)
It is not too late
—turn to life,
God is in your heart:
when you stop fleeing
    death
life rises in you,
when you face the dark
    ahead
light flows down on you,
and when you take up your
    loneliness
love comes to you
inside your heart,
and that is God
in you,
the same as God is
in the universe.

Dance of the Spirits

O Light / Eternal Vision
    (Round)

Spell (*Joana*) / **Prayer**
    (*Santo Antonio*)
(*Joana*) Santatonho
    catungado
Ere mora na aruana
E vem casa fia de ubana.
Sant'Antonio, your house is
    in heaven,

but you come to earth
to marry off us daughters of
  the earth.
Santatonho catungado
Ere mora na aruana
E vem casa fia de ubana.
Sant'Antonio, your house is
  in heaven,
but you come to earth
to marry off us daughters of
  the earth.
(*Santo Antonio*) O light, be
  in my mind,
and in my understanding!
O light, be in my eyes,
and in my looking!
O light, be in my mouth,
and in my speaking!
O light, be in my heart,
and in my thinking!
(*Joana*) O light, be at my
  end,
and at my departing!

You are in love (*Joana*)
You are in love
with Holy Wisdom,
with pure spirit,
but I am all too aware
of being in a body,
and of indwelling,
and of time going in circles,
never standing

still and peaceful like
  eternity,
and yet there is a way
I know between us, Yes
  between us,
to dance with all your heart,
to dance with all your soul,
to dance with all your
  might.

Wisdom
(*Santo Antonio* and *Joana*)
Wisdom is
to have a heart
according to God's heart,
for life is always saying
"Ask what I shall give you
—anyone and anything
your heart desires can be."
Say "an understanding
  mind"
—everyone and everything
will be yours in letting be,
you will be in openness
to all their mystery,
and God's eyes and God's
  heart
will be there for all time.

We have been there
(*Antonio* and *Cordolina*)
We have been there
where fear is passing

—We have been there
where love is lasting
on the turning wheel of
    memory,
always returning
things and situations
meant to be the signs
of ways into the heart,
for as the wheel does turn
the center moves in forward
    love,
the end of everlasting fears
and the beginning of
    unbounded hopes
of all we ever loved.

Time's Arrow (*Cordolina*)
Time's arrow
becomes love's direction,
—for my striving
becomes prayer
and sensible to life in
    death,
to light in darkness,

and to love in lovelessness,
—for who is poor?
and who is devil?
—for God answered
even Christ's prayer
in his agony
by taking will
and giving peace.

O Light (*Chorus*)
O light
before me
and behind me,
on my right
and on my left!
O light,
where are you?
I am lost,
show me the way!
O light,
shine on
divided heart,
and wandering eye,
and my poor devil's cry!

THE GOLDEN KEY

Prelude

First Act

The Golden Key
(*Mossy and his Great Aunt*)
At rainbow's end
there is a golden key,
but what does it lock
or unlock for me?
What can I know
of heart's desire?
What should I do?
What may I hope?
Is death the key
to our true happiness?
Yet do not seek death,
death will find you,
seek instead the road
of lasting love.

Rainbow Song (1)
(*Mossy and Chorus*)
Inside my heart I see
the rainbow bridge
from earth to heaven,
and my heart leaps up
with intimations of eternal
    life,
as if the rainbow gave
our spirit its rebirth

in broken light,
for incandescent is the
    spirit
that is pure of heart
and wills one thing,
but iridescent is the spirit
that is heart and soul
in love with all.

Rainbow Dance
(*Mossy and Chorus*)
I can see
the rainbow in my heart
when all my eyes see
is the dark.

A Night in the Forest
    (*Tangle*)
My soul dwells
in a haunted house of souls
and is alone and does not
    know
until I run away
and see a flying fish of light
to guide me and to guard
    me
from a groping tree of dark
and lead me to the lighted
    doorway
of a heaven haven
where a lady dwells

in beauty we can know
and know unknown, dark
  lady
and eternal friend of
  knowing
and unknowing love.

Cycle Song (*Lady in the
  Forest*)
We live all in a cycle,
coming young into the air
and growing old outside the
  water,
going down into the earth
and into fire to be reborn
as ancient children
who can learn from the
  beginning
to pronounce the word of
  life
and sing and dance eternal
  music,
for we live each other's death
and we die each other's life,
but if you lose each other,
do not be afraid, go on and
  on.

The Golden Key
  (Reprise)
(*Mossy*) At rainbow's end
I found a golden key,
and where I go now

will you come with me?
(*Tangle*) What can we
  know
of heart's desire?
What should we do?
What may we hope?
(*Lady*) We become all the
  things
we know and love,
and so we live each other's
  death
and we die each other's life.
(*Mossy and Tangle*) Is death
  the key
to our true happiness?
(*Lady*) Yet do not seek death,
death will find you,
seek instead the road
of lasting love,
and if you lose each other,
do not be afraid, go on and
  on.

Walking Song (*Mossy and
  Tangle*)
If you are ready to let go
of everyone and everything
you want and cannot have,
to let there be light
and be open to the dark
  unknown,
if you are free and
  heart-free,

you are ready for a walk,
for long ago we understood
the very songs of birds
and were as free ourselves,
but now we have to learn
    again
the way of all the earth,
to sing and dance
upon the mystic road.

Shadow Song (*Mossy and
    Tangle*)
Can I leap over
my own shadow
fleeing from me
as I age and pass away,
yet walking with me,
striding after me,
and rising up to meet me?
Yes, though I walk lonely
through the hidden valley
of the shadowland
of death my death,
I fear no evil,
for you are there with me,
and you comfort me.

Shadow Dance
(*Mossy, Tangle, and Chorus*)
I leap over
my own shadow
and it leaps on
into mystery.

Second Act

Wind Spirit Song
(*Lady as Wind Spirit*)
Unless you come of water
and the wind,
you cannot come there
where divine wind blows
of dying and of birthing,
for your flesh is flesh,
and spirit is your spirit,
so you come again,
and when the wind is
    blowing
where it wills,
the wind harp sings,
and you can hear the
    sound
of Aeolian music
from unknown to the
    unknown.

The Old Man of the Sea
(*Old Man*) My heart is with
    the sea,
and I will dwell along this
    shore
until the last ship sails,
for I have waited here for
    you.
(*Tangle*) All I see of you is
    old
except your eyes,

and they are of the color of
the sea,
and they are cheerful,
undefeated.
(*Old Man*) All I see of you is
beautiful
except your eyes
are troubled,
they are restless till you find
repose in heart's desire.
(*Tangle*) My heart is restless
till I find the land
from which the shadows fall,
the land of heart's desire.
Will you show me the way
to find the land of heart's
desire?

Sea Song
(*Tangle and Chorus*)
We listen to our inmost
selves,
and we do not know
which sea we hear
murmuring,
the overwhelming sweep,
the vastness,
—for who can tell the soul
from God within
if soul is made for God,
unless it be by darkness
of the waters stirred by
wind,

unless it be by light,
strange light upon the sea,
still more mysterious
than darkness of the soul.

The Old Man of the Earth
(*Old Man*) Yes, I am old,
No, I am young,
for I look in the mirror
of our scorn and pity,
and I know it is a looking
glass
where we see darkly now,
but then when we are face-
to-face
and seeing light
of eyes we cannot see
in self-portrayal,
posing for ourselves,
but only in the eyes of love,
we shall know then
as we are known.

Earth Song
(*Tangle and Chorus*)
Living in uncertainty
without despairing,
we live in earth's mystery
that shows itself
and then withdraws,
earth's shadow
rising to the zenith
as the sun is setting,

and we rise to follow after
One who is to come
in presence
of time out of mind
upon the way of change
of life and longing into love.

The Ancient Child
(*Old Man*) Sing
and dance
around the circle,
for your labors will be
    heavy,
but divine fire
will support you
in the weariness you've
    taken on,
the cry of heart
inside a heartless world,
the soul of soulless life gone
    cold,
but you will kindle and
    rekindle
all the passion of deep life,
as heat becomes as light,
illumining the heart.

Fire Song
(*Tangle and Chorus*)
Time
is pastime,
is a child

at play
with fire
to kindle
and illumine
human hearts
by words
of music
in dark ages,
for a song
and dance
of light.

Circle Dance of Light
(*Tangle and Chorus*)
Light flows down
in circles eye to eye
and heart to heart
upon love's road.

Night Sea Journey (*Mossy*)
Am I resting
now in restlessness
and growing young again
as I look for a seaway to the
    land
from which the shadows fall,
a rainbow passage over
    waters
where you taste your death
and think it better than life
when it is only more life?
—but I see the rainbow,

and this is indeed my way,
a night sea journey,
opposite the sun,
and to the farthest shore!

Meeting after Life
(*Mossy and Tangle*)
(*Mossy*) Here is where the
    living
meet the dead and live
    again,
the alcove where you meet
again the ones you love,
and here I meet again the
    one
I always loved and lost,
all lovely and all still and
    peaceful.
(*Tangle*) I have waited for
    you
long, long! But you, you
are like the old, the young,
the ancient child!
Yet you are my own old
    friend,
and love has changed us
into all the things we love!

Rainbow Song (2) (*Mossy and Tangle*)
In the end is the Word
as in the beginning,
for we saw only a fog bow,
just a moonbow,
a white rainbow,
but now we see inner light,
and we are on a winding
    stair
inside the rainbow,
and all hues of being
climb along with us,
and we ascend we know
into a land of heart's desire,
for we can hear the music
of a word beyond all speech.

Rainbow Dance (*All*)
I can see
the rainbow in my heart
when all my eyes see
is the dark.

Notes

Preface

1. Paul Auster has a novel called *The Music of Chance* (New York: Viking, 1990), and Anthony Powell has a series of twelve novels in four volumes called *A Dance to the Music of Time* (Chicago: University of Chicago Press, 1995), named after Nicolas Poussin's painting "A Dance to the Music of Time" (c. 1639–40) and modeled after Marcel Proust's *Remembrance of Things Past*.

2. Shakespeare, *All's Well That Ends Well*, act 1, scene 3, line 179 in W. J. Craig, ed., *The Oxford Shakespeare* (London: Oxford University Press, 1957), p. 274.

3. T. E. Lawrence, *Seven Pillars of Wisdom* (Harmondsworth, England: Penguin and Jonathan Cape, 1971), p. 364. See below my discussion in "Of Time and the Ecstasy of Being Ever."

4. Shakespeare, *All's Well That Ends Well*, act 4, scene 4, line 35, and act 5, scene 1, line 25, in *The Oxford Shakespeare*, pp. 292 and 293.

5. Wilhelm Grimm and Maurice Sendak (illustrations), *Dear Mili* (New York: Farrar Straus & Giroux, 1988) (pages not numbered). See my discussion below in "Of Time and the Ecstasy of Being Ever" and "Between Heart and Heart" and "The Heart of Mystery."

6. Kathleen Norris, *Dakota* (New York: Ticknor & Fields, 1993), p. 102. See my discussion below in "The Heart of Mystery."

7. F. E. Hutchinson, ed., *The Works of George Herbert* (Oxford: Clarendon, 1964), p. 354 ("Outlandish Proverbs" #1006).

8. Shakespeare, *Hamlet*, act 3, scene 2, prose after line 366, in *The Oxford Shakespeare*, p. 890.

The Music of Time

1. *The Road Goes Ever On: A Song Cycle*, poems by J. R. R. Tolkien, music by Donald Swann (Boston: Houghton Mifflin, 1967).

2. The old man's name was Anthony Cima, and his photograph and his story are in an article by Jerry Griswold in the *Los Angeles Times* for Sunday, February 13, 1994, pp. 1 and 15 of the Book Review section.

3. William Nicholson is the author of both the play, *Shadowlands* (New York: Penguin, 1991), and the screenplay (1994), but this line occurs only in the screenplay.

4. Franz Schubert, *Shorter Works for Pianoforte Solo* (New York: Dover, 1970), pp. 170–89. See O. E. Deutsch, *Schubert Thematic Catalogue* (New York: Norton, 1950), p. 205 (#459).

5. Martin Heidegger, *Discourse on Thinking*, a translation of his *Gelassenheit* by John M. Anderson and E. Hans Freund (New York: Harper & Row, 1966), p. 55.

6. Jean Vanier received the Notre Dame Award on April 18, 1994, at the Stepan Center at Notre Dame. See his book *Be Not Afraid* (New York: Paulist, 1975).

7. Albert Einstein as quoted by Abraham Pais in his biography of Einstein, *Subtle Is the Lord: The Science and Life of Albert Einstein* (New York: Oxford University Press, 1982), p. 468.

8. This is the full title of *The Cloud of Unknowing* quoted by Clifton Wolters in his edition of *The Cloud of Unknowing and Other Works* (New York: Penguin, 1978), p. 46.

9. George Tyrrell as quoted by Frans Jozef van Beeck in Jeffrey Carlson and Robert A. Ludwig, eds., *Jesus and Faith* (Maryknoll, N.Y.: Orbis, 1994), p. 98, note 8.

10. See my discussion of this formula in *The Peace of the Present* (Notre Dame and London: University of Notre Dame Press, 1991), p. 101.

11. Franz Kafka, *The Great Wall of China*, trans. Willa and Edwin Muir (New York: Schocken, 1946). I substitute the word "striving" for "effort," following Nahum Glatzer in his *Language of Faith* (New York: Schocken, 1967), p. 35. See my discussion of this saying in *The Homing Spirit* (New York: Crossroad, 1987), p. 39.

12. Saint John of the Cross, *Dark Night of the Soul*, trans. E. Allison Peers (New York: Doubleday, 1959), p. 34.

13. Milan Kundera, *Immortality*, a novel, trans. Peter Kussi (New York: Grove, 1991), pp. 40 and 61.

14. J. R. R. Tolkien, *The Lord of the Rings* (London: Allen & Unwin, 1969), p. 87.

15. Proverbs 29:18 (KJ).

16. "Das Ewigweibliche zieht uns hinan!" This is the last sentence of Goethe's *Faust*. I am using Kussi's translation in Kundera's *Immortality*, p. 341.

A Memory Theatre

1. A proverb quoted by Ted Hughes, *Shakespeare and the Goddess of Complete Being* (New York: Farrar, Straus & Giroux, 1992), p. 159.

2. George MacDonald, *The Golden Key* (New York: Farrar, Straus & Giroux, 1976), p. 78 (happy ending), p. 34 (Lady's advice), p. 45 (Tangle remembers the advice).

3. Ibid., p. 78.

4. Meister Eckhart quoted by Martin Heidegger, *Poetry, Language, Thought*, trans. Albert Hofstadter (New York: Harper & Row, 1971), p. 176.

5. See Francis A. Yates, *The Art of Memory* (Chicago: University of Chicago Press, 1966), especially chapter VI and chapter XVI and the foldout between pp. 144 and 145.

6. Cicero quoted by Etienne Gilson, *Heloise and Abelard*, trans. L. K. Shook (London: Hollis & Carter, 1953), p. 57 ("omnis ejus fructus in ipso amore est").

7. Aristotle, *De Anima*, Book III, 431b21 (my translation). See my discussion in "St. Thomas' Theology of Participation" in *Theological Studies*, vol. 18, no. 4 (December 1957), pp. 506–12.

8. J. R. R. Tolkien, *The Lord of the Rings* (London: Allen & Unwin, 1969), p. 703.

9. See the prayer in Ignatius Esser, *The Chapter Room of Saint Meinrad Archabbey* (St. Meinrad, Ind.: Grail, 1955), p. 17 : "Almighty and eternal God, who hast taught our holy Father Benedict to behold the entire world in one ray of the sun and hast symbolized to him in the splendor of gleaming light the joys of heavenly life, we beg thee to enlighten our minds with the symbols of the Holy Rule shown in these windows and to fill our hearts with the desire of seeing thee, through Christ our Lord. Amen." On "design by accident" see James Francis O'Brien, *Design by Accident* (New York: Dover, 1968), on using patterns in nature to create designs.

10. I want to suggest the scientific vision in the one phrase, "light can be both wave and particle," though it is also the title of Ellen Gilchrist's story that I quote below in note 29, and I want to suggest the religious vision in the other phrase, "in the splendor of gleaming light the joys of heavenly life," that I quote from the prayer in note 9.

11. John 4:24 (RSV).

12. Yates, *The Art of Memory*, pp. 257–58.

13. Julia Kristeva, *Tales of Love*, trans. Leon S. Roudiez (New York: Columbia University Press, 1987), p. 1.

14. W. B. Yeats, *A Vision* (New York: Collier, 1966), p. 83.

15. Diana Friel McGowin, *Living in the Labyrinth: A Personal Journey through the Maze of Alzheimer's* (San Francisco: Elder Books, 1993).

16. Saint Augustine, *Confessions*, trans. Henry Chadwick (Oxford: Oxford University Press, 1991), p. 191 (Book X, chapter 14).

17. William Wordsworth, "Preface to Lyrical Ballads" in *William Wordsworth*, ed. Stephen Gill (Oxford and New York: Oxford University Press, 1990), p. 611.

18. From George Herbert's poem "The Call" in F. E. Hutchinson, ed., *The Works of George Herbert* (Oxford: Clarendon, 1941), p. 156.

19. Augustine, *Confessions*, p. 3 (Book I, chapter 1).

20. Leo Bersani amd Ulysse Dutoit, *The Forms of Violence* (New York: Schocken, 1985), p. 125.

21. Augustine, *Confessions*, p. 201 (Book X, chapter 27).

22. *The Notebooks of Joseph Joubert*, ed. and trans. Paul Auster, with an Afterword by Maurice Blanchot, trans. Lydia Davis (San Francisco: North Point, 1983), pp. 180–81.

23. Theodor Adorno, *Kierkegaard*, trans. Robert Hullot-Kentor (Minneapolis: University of Minnesota Press, 1989), p. 140. See my discussion in *The Peace of the Present*, pp. 73–74 and 79.

24. Michael Perlman, *Imaginal Memory and the Place of Hiroshima* (Albany: State University of New York Press, 1988), p. 128.

25. Joao Ubaldo Ribeiro, *An Invincible Memory* (New York: Harper & Row, 1989), epigraph.

26. Martin Buber, *Ecstatic Confessions*, ed. Paul Mendes-Flohr, trans. Esther Cameron (San Francisco: Harper & Row, 1985), p. 11.

27. The subtitle of George Crumb's *Makrokosmos* is "Twelve Fantasy Pieces after the Zodiac" (New York: Peters, 1973 and 1974). The chapter room of the abbey I visited is the one described by Ignatius Esser cited above in note 9. The three principles I am using here, "the two worlds are really one," "figure and ground can be reversed," and "the whole is more than a sum of parts" are from Murray Cox and Alice Thielgaard, *Mutative Metaphors in Psychotherapy* (London: Tavistock, 1987), p. x (see my discussion in *The Peace of the Present*, p. 47).

28. It is the direction Beethoven writes over the Kyrie of his *Missa Solemnis* (Opus 123 in D major).

29. Ellen Gilchrist, *Light Can Be Both Wave and Particle* (Boston, Toronto and London: Little, Brown and Co., 1989), p. 66 (I am quoting here from the title story in this book of stories).

30. Isak Dinesen (Karen Blixen), *Anecdotes of Destiny* (New York: Vintage, 1985), p. 60.

31. Ibid., pp. 62–63.

32. Søren Kierkegaard, *The Sickness unto Death* (published with *Fear and Trembling*), trans. Walter Lowrie (Garden City, N.Y.: Doubleday, 1954), pp. 173–74. See my discussion in *Reasons of the Heart* (New York: Macmillan, 1978; rpt. Notre Dame, Ind.: University of Notre Dame Press, 1979), pp. 25–31.

33. Dinesen, *Anecdotes of Destiny*, p. 68.

34. Leon Bloy, *Pilgrim of the Absolute*, selections by Raissa Maritain, trans. John Coleman and Harry Lorin Binsse (New York: Pantheon, 1947), p. 349. See my discussion in *The Peace of the Present*, p. 103.

35. Baal Shem Tov quoted by Shamai Kanter in *Cross Currents*, vol. 41, no. 3 (Fall 1991), p. 353 (see my response there on p. 376).

36. Pascal, *Pensées*, #474 (my translation)—I am using the edition by Jacques Chevalier in Pascal, *Oeuvres Completes* (Paris: Gallimard, Bibliotheque de la Pleiade, 1954), p. 1221. See my discussion in *Reasons of the Heart*, p. xii and throughout that book.

37. "Child's Way" is from my song cycle "Ayasofya" in the appendix of my book *Love's Mind* (Notre Dame: University of Notre Dame Press, 1993).

38. Dag Hammarskjöld, "A Room of Quiet" (New York: United Nations, 1971), opening sentence.

39. Meister Eckhart quoted by William James, *The Varieties of Religious Experience* (New York: Mentor, 1958), p. 320.

40. John 17:23 (KJ and RSV).

41. Meister Eckhart, *Parisian Questions and Prologues*, trans. Armand A. Maurer (Toronto: Pontifical Institute of Medieval Studies, 1974), pp. 85–86. The Latin sentence is *Esse est Deus*—see

Meister Eckhart, *Die Lateinischen Werke*, ed. Konrad Weiss, vol. 1 (Stuttgart: W. Kohlhammer, 1964), p. 38. See my discussion in *The House of Wisdom* (San Francisco: Harper & Row, 1985; rpt. Notre Dame: University of Notre Dame Press, 1993), p. 3.

42. See above, note 18. Ralph Vaughan Williams set this poem to music in "Five Mystical Songs" (September 14, 1911).

43. Ephesians 3:17 (KJ).

44. See John Henry Newman, *Apologia Pro Vita Sua*, ed. Martin J. Svaglic (Oxford: Clarendon, 1967), p. 177, and Plotinus, *Enneads*, Book VI, chapter 9 at end in *Plotinus*, trans. A. H. Armstrong, vol. 7 (Cambridge, Mass.: Harvard University Press, 1988), p. 344 (Armstrong translates "escape in solitude to the solitary" but notes that the usual translation is "flight of the alone to the Alone").

45. See Leon Langlet, *L'Eglise esoterique de Planes* (Pyrenees orientales)(Perpignan: Imprimerie du Midi, 1966).

46. Le Corbusier (Edouard Jeanneret-Gris), *The Chapel at Ronchamp* (New York: Frederick A. Praeger, 1957), p. 95. See my discussion in *The Church of the Poor Devil* (New York: Macmillan, 1982; rpt. Notre Dame: University of Notre Dame Press, 1983), p. 39. I say "circular shape of the Ayasofya" but it would be more accurate to say "a circle between two semicircles inside a square." See my discussion of these places in *The House of Wisdom* and *The Church of the Poor Devil*.

47. See Gustave Flaubert, *La Tentation de saint Antoine*, ed. Edouard Maynial (Paris: Garnier, 1954), p. 276.

48. Helen Luke, "Choices in the Lord of the Rings" (unpublished essay quoted with permission of the author).

49. Jean-Pierre de Caussade, *Abandonment to Divine Providence*, trans. John Beevers (New York: Doubleday, 1975).

50. See Gilbert Keith Chesterton, *Collected Works*, vol. 2 (San Francisco: Ignatius Press, 1986), pp. 29–30 (Saint Francis in love), and pp. 495–512 ("The Real Life of Saint Thomas").

51. Martin Heidegger, *Discourse on Thinking*, a translation of his *Gelassenheit* by John M. Anderson and E. Hans Freund (New York: Harper & Row, 1966), p. 55. I am translating the word *Gelassenheit*

here as "letting be" rather than "releasement." See my discussion of "letting be" and "openness to the mystery" in *The Peace of the Present*, pp. 10 and 18 (comparing and contrasting Eckhart and Heidegger).

Of Time and the Ecstasy of Being Ever

1. Alan Lightman, *Einstein's Dreams* (New York: Pantheon, 1993), p. 52.

2. 2 Peter 3:8 (KJ).

3. Martin Heidegger, *The Concept of Time*, English-German edition, trans. William McNeill (Cambridge, Mass.: Blackwell, 1992), p. 22E.

4. Samuel Barber, *The Prayers of Kierkegaard*, Opus 30 (New York: Schirmer, 1955), text facing p.1 (trans. not mentioned), these words set to music on pp. 22–26.

5. Julian of Norwich, *Showings*, trans. Edmund Colledge and James Walsh (New York: Paulist, 1978), p. 318 (seventy-first chapter in the Long Text).

6. Tolkien, *The Lord of the Rings*, p. 76.

7. Sir Thomas Browne, *Urne Buriall and the Garden of Cyrus*, ed. John Carter (Cambridge at the University Press, 1967), p. 50.

8. Ludwig Wittgenstein, *Tractatus Logico-Philosophicus*, English-German edition, trans. D. F. Pears and B. F. McGuinness (London: Routledge & Kegan Paul, 1961), p. 147 (proposition #6.4311).

9. John 6:68 (KJ and RSV).

10. Tolkien at the end of his essay "On Fairy Stories" in *The Tolkien Reader* (New York: Ballantine, 1991), p. 89.

11. Peter Maxwell Davies, *Leopardi Fragments* (London: Schott, 1965), pp. 33–36. The words are sung in the original Italian. The translation here is mine. (A translation by Nigel Fortune is given at the beginning of the score.)

12. T. E. Lawrence, *Seven Pillars of Wisdom*, p. 364. See my discussion in *Reasons of the Heart*, p. 1.

13. Plato, *Timaeus*, 37d (my translation).

14. Miguel de Cervantes, *Don Quixote*, trans. J. M. Cohen (New York: Penguin, 1950), p. 54 ("I know who I am") and p. 434 ("I most certainly know that I am enchanted").

15. John 8:14 (RSV).

16. Cervantes, *Don Quixote*, p. 938.

17. Miguel de Unamuno, *The Tragic Sense of Life*, trans. J. E. Crawford Futch (New York: Dover, 1954), p. 297.

18. T. S. Eliot, *Four Quartets* (New York: Harcourt, Brace & World, 1943), p. 14 ("East Coker").

19. Cervantes, *Don Quixote*, p. 938.

20. Marcel Proust, *On Reading*, bilingual text ed. and trans. Jean Autret and William Burford (New York: Macmillan, 1971), p. 31.

21. Tolkien at the end of his essay "On Fairy Stories" in *The Tolkien Reader*, p. 89.

22. Franz Kafka, *The Great Wall of China*, trans. Willa and Edwin Muir, p. 306 (aphorism #101).

23. Tolkien, *The Lord of the Rings*, p. 48 (see also pp. 86 and 1024), and see his song cycle, *The Road Goes Ever On*, music by Donald Swann, poems by J. R. R. Tolkien (Boston: Houghton Mifflin, 1967).

24. *The Collected Poems of Wallace Stevens* (New York: Knopf, 1976), p. 524. I am grateful to John T. Noonan, Jr., for showing me this poem.

25. John Henry Newman, *Prose and Poetry*, ed. George N. Shuster (New York: Allyn & Bacon, 1925), p. 116.

26. Newman, *Apologia Pro Vita Sua* (New York: Modern Library, 1950), p. 62.

27. Diogenes' description of Plato's philosophy in *Herakleitos and Diogenes*, trans. Guy Davenport (San Francisco: Grey Fox, 1983), p. 47 (aphorism #47).

28. *The Soliloquies of Saint Augustine*, trans. Rose Elizabeth Cleveland (Boston: Little, Brown, 1910), p. 10 (Book I, chapter II), p. 51 (Book II, chapter I), and p. 65 (Book II, chapter VI). I have modified the translations slightly to reflect the parallelism of *me* and *te* in the Latin.

29. Heidegger, "The Way Back into the Ground of Metaphysics," trans. Walter Kaufmann, *Existentialism from Dostoevsky to Sartre* (New York: New American Library, 1975), p. 270.

30. Kafka, *Tagebucher* (New York: Schocken, 1949), p. 475 (my translation). See my discussion of this passage in *Reasons of the Heart*, p. 5, and in *The House of Wisdom*, pp. 129–30, and in *Love's Mind*, p. 38.

31. John 17:23 (KJ and RSV).

32. Walter Benjamin, *Illuminations*, ed. Hannah Arendt, trans. Harry Zohn (New York: Schocken, 1969), p. 134.

33. Plato, *Theatetus*, 172e (my translation). Theodorus says this to Socrates who takes up the idea a few lines further on.

34. Heidegger in his preface to William J. Richardson, *Heidegger: Through Phenomenology to Thought* (The Hague: M. Nijhoff, 1963), p. xx.

35. Frederic Prokosch (trans.), *Some Poems of Friedrich Hölderlin* (Norfolk, Conn.: New Directions, 1943) (pages not numbered).

36. John 1:1–5 (RSV).

37. Prokosch in his "Biographical Note" at the beginning of *Some Poems of Friedrich Hölderlin*.

38. John 8:12 (my translation).

39. Henri Huvelin, *Some Spiritual Guides of the Seventeenth Century*, trans. Joseph Leonard (New York: Benziger, 1927), p. 68.

40. Sanhedrin 106b. See my discussion in *The Peace of the Present*, p. 18 and note 46 on p. 117.

41. Heidegger, *Being and Time*, trans. John Macquarrie and Edward Robinson (New York: Harper & Bros., 1962), p. 311.

42. Dag Hammarskjöld, *Markings*, trans. Leif Sjöberg and W. H. Auden (New York: Knopf, 1964), p. 90.

43. Saint Augustine, *Homilies on I John*, VIIth Homily, in Augustine, *Later Works*, trans. John Burnaby (Philadelphia: Westminster, 1955), p. 316.

44. Chesterton, *Collected Works*, vol. 2, p. 501.

45. See my discussion of Saint Thomas's prayer "Nothing, Lord, but you" in *The House of Wisdom*, p. 16. On his reaching a

point of vision beyond words see Josef Pieper, *The Silence of Saint Thomas* (New York: Pantheon, 1957).

46. Nicholas of Cusa, *The Vision of God*, trans. Emma Gurney Salter (New York: Ungar, 1969). See my discussion in *Reasons of the Heart*, pp. 39–40.

47. Leo Tolstoy, *The Death of Ivan Ilych*, trans. Aylmer Maude (New York: New American Library, 1960), p. 156.

48. Spinoza, *Ethics*, Book V, proposition #19 and proposition #36 (corollary) in Spinoza, *Opera* (Heidelberg: Carl Winters, 1972), vol. 2, pp. 292 and 302 (my translation).

49. *Webster's Dictionary of Synonyms* (Springfield, Mass.: G. & C. Merriam, 1951), p. 834.

50. Novalis as quoted by Etienne Gilson, *God and Philosophy* (New Haven: Yale University Press, 1941), p. 102. See Novalis, *Pollen and Fragments*, trans. Arthur Versluis (Grand Rapids, Mich.: Phanes, 1989), p. 123.

51. "Sed omnia praeclara tam difficilia, quam rara sunt" in Spinoza, *Opera*, vol. 2, p. 308. I am using Stephen Mitchell's translation of this sentence in his *Parables and Portraits* (New York: Harper & Row, 1990), p. 47.

52. Wendell Berry, *The Wheel* (San Francisco: North Point, 1982), p. 26.

53. John 9:4 (KJ).

54. Saint John of the Cross, *Dark Night of the Soul*, p. 34.

55. Wilhelm Grimm and Maurice Sendak (illustrations), *Dear Mili* (New York: Farrar Straus & Giroux, 1988) (pages not numbered). The discovery of this tale was reported on the front page of the *New York Times* on September 28, 1983.

56. This is the full title of *The Cloud of Unknowing*. See Clifton Wolters, ed., *The Cloud of Unknowing and Other Works*, p. 46.

57. Abraham Pais, *Subtle Is the Lord*, p. 17.

58. Aeschylus, *Agamemnon*, lines 177 and 250 (my translation). I am using the Greek-English edition in the Loeb Classical Library, *Aeschylus*, ed. and trans. Hebert Weir Smyth, vol. 2 (Cambridge, Mass.: Harvard University Press, 1957), pp. 18 and 22.

Between Heart and Heart

1. Tolkien, *The Lord of the Rings*, p. 499.

2. This is from Richard Rorty's comment on the book jacket of James C. Edwards, *The Authority of Language* (Tampa: University of South Florida, 1990).

3. Jacob and Wilhelm Grimm, "The Three Languages," in David M. Guss, *The Language of the Birds* (San Francisco: North Point, 1985), pp. 103–5.

4. Thomas Mann, *The Holy Sinner*, trans. H. T. Lowe-Porter (New York: Knopf, 1951). For an illuminating interpretation of the story see John Perkins, *The Forbidden Self* (Boston and London: Shambala, 1992).

5. Michael Polanyi, *The Tacit Dimension* (Gloucester, Mass.: Peter Smith, 1983), p. 4.

6. Olivier Messiaen, *Quatuor pour la Fin du Temps* (Paris: Durand, 1942), p. i (my translation).

7. I am quoting here from the program notes for the performance by the Berkeley Symphony Orchestra, Kent Nagano conducting, on August 25, 1993.

8. Hermann Broch, *The Death of Virgil*, trans. Jean Starr Untermeyer (San Francisco: North Point, 1983), p. 482.

9. John 2:25 (KJ).

10. See my discussion of "I am" in *The Peace of the Present*, pp. 93–95.

11. Dag Hammarskjöld, "A Room of Quiet" (New York: United Nations, 1971), concluding sentence.

12. A. N. Whitehead, *Adventures of Ideas* (New York: Macmillan, 1937), p. 14. See my discussion in *A Search for God in Time and Memory* (New York: Macmillan, 1969; rpt. Notre Dame: University of Notre Dame Press, 1977), p. 33.

13. I began using the term "passing over" in my second book, *A Search for God in Time and Memory*, but the process is already there in my first book, *The City of the Gods* (New York: Macmillan, 1965; rpt. Notre Dame: University of Notre Dame Press, 1978),

where I see life opening up to death and begin to pass over into ways of life and death.

14. Here again I am quoting from the full title of *The Cloud of Unknowing*. See above, "The Music of Time," note 8.

15. Tolkien, *The Lord of the Rings*, p. 1122.

16. Michel Poizat, *The Angel's Cry*, trans. Arthur Denner (Ithaca and London: Cornell University Press, 1992).

17. Ludwig Wittgenstein, *Tractatus Logico-Philosophicus*, trans. D. F. Pears and B. F. McGuinness, p. 151 (#7).

18. Wittgenstein, *Philosophical Investigations*, trans. G. E. M. Anscombe (New York: Macmillan, 1968), p. 143e (Part I, #527).

19. Søren Kierkegaard, *Concluding Unscientific Postscript*, trans. David Swenson and Walter Lowrie (Princeton: Princeton University Press, 1941), p. 311.

20. Messiaen, *Quatuor pour la Fin du Temps*, p. i, "il n'y aura plus de Temps," quoting Revelation 10:6, "that there should be time no longer" (KJ).

21. John 1:14 (KJ).

22. T. S. Eliot, *Four Quartets* (New York: Harcourt Brace Jovanovich, 1988), p. 44 ("The Dry Salvages," line 215).

23. Ibid., line 201.

24. Ibid., lines 211–12.

25. Beethoven, Opus 135 (String Quartet in F major). I am using the Philharmonica edition (Vienna: Wiener Philharmonischer Verlag, 1936), p. 20. See Milan Kundera's discussion of these words in his novel *The Unbearable Lightness of Being*, trans. by Michael Henry Heim (New York: Harper Perennial, 1991), pp. 32–35 and p. 195. See my discussion in *Love's Mind*, p. 36.

26. This song, called "One," is from my song cycle "Ayaso-fya" in the appendix of *Love's Mind*, p. 125. On waking, dreaming, dreamless sleep, and the One (=Atman) see the Mandukya Upanishad in Juan Mascaro, trans., *The Upanishads* (New York: Penguin, 1965), pp. 83–84.

27. Paul Griffiths, *Olivier Messiaen and the Music of Time* (Ithaca, N.Y.: Cornell University Press, 1985), p. 15.

28. Alcmaeon, Fragment 2, trans. Kathleen Freeman in *Ancilla to the Pre-Socratic Philosophers* (Cambridge, Mass.: Harvard University Press, 1957), p. 40. See my discussion in *The Church of the Poor Devil*, p. 23.

29. Heraclitus, Fragment 16, in *Ancilla to the Pre-Socratic Philosophers*, p. 26.

30. Sigmund Freud, *Beyond the Pleasure Principle*, trans. James Strachey (New York: Bantam, 1963), p. 54.

31. "By believing I could have been healed. My mind's eye thus purified would have been directed in some degree towards your truth which abides forever and is indefectible," he says in his *Confessions*, p. 95 (Book VI, chapter 4). See the texts of Augustine assembled by F. Moriones in his *Enchiridion Theologicum Sancti Augustini* (Madrid: B.A.C., 1961), under the heading "Crede ut intelligas," pp. 14–19.

32. See my discussion of "the new name" in *The Peace of the Present*, pp. 6–8.

33. Virgil, *Aeneid*, Book VI, lines 893–98. I am using the Loeb edition by H. R. Fairclough (Cambridge, Mass.: Harvard University Press, 1960), pp. 570–71.

34. Humphrey Carpenter, *Tolkien* (Boston: Houghton Mifflin, 1977), p. 147.

35. Tolkien at the end of his essay "On Fairy Stories" in *The Tolkien Reader*, pp. 89–90.

36. Tolkien, *The Lord of the Rings*, p. 982.

37. See my conversation with David Daube on "I am" in *The Peace of the Present*, pp. 93–95.

38. John 9:9 and John 18:17 and 25 (KJ).

39. Manuel y Antonio Machado, *Obras Completas* (Madrid: Plenitud, 1967), p. 837 (my translation). See Robert Bly's trans. in Antonio Machado, *I Never Wanted Fame* (St. Paul, Minn.: Ally, 1979), #VI (no page numbers).

40. T. S. Eliot, *The Three Voices of Poetry* (New York: Cambridge University Press, 1954).

41. T. S. Eliot, *Four Quartets*, pp. 23 and 32 (the first line and the last line of "East Coker").

42. Ibid., p. 32 (phrases from the last lines of "East Coker").

43. Saint Francis of Assisi, "The Canticle for Brother Sun," trans. Jerome Rothenberg in Guss, *The Language of the Birds*, pp. 243–44.

44. Griffiths, *Olivier Messiaen and the Music of Time*, p. 240.

45. Ibid., p. 239.

46. See my discussion of this saying in *The Peace of the Present*, p. 50.

This World's a City Full of Straying Streets

1. Novalis (Friedrich von Hardenberg), *The Novices of Sais*, trans. Ralph Manheim (New York: Curt Valentin, 1949), p. 3.

2. This is the basic question posed in my first book, *The City of the Gods*.

3. Charles O. Hartman, *Jazz Text* (Princeton: Princeton University Press, 1991), p. 9.

4. This song is called "Inside a Song" and is from my song cycle *Songs about Songs* in *Love's Mind*, pp. 135–36.

5. Shakespeare and Fletcher, *Two Noble Kinsmen*, act 1, scene 5, lines 16–17. I am using *The Oxford Shakespeare*, ed. by Eugene M. Waith (Oxford: Clarendon, 1989), p. 106.

6. Son House quoted by Jeff Todd Titon, "The Life Story" in *Journal of American Folklore* 90 (1980), p. 279.

7. I am echoing Stephen Spender's description of Rimbaud in his preface to Novalis, *The Novices of Sais*, p. vii. See Arthur Rimbaud, *A Season in Hell and The Drunken Boat*, trans. Louise Varese (New York: New Directions, 1961).

8. Dante, *Inferno*, Canto 3, line 9 (my trans.). I am using the Temple edition, *Dante's Inferno* (London: Dent, 1962), p. 26.

9. Bruce Chatwin, *The Songlines* (New York: Penguin, 1988), p. 19.

10. Ibid., p. 64.

11. Ibid., p. 108.

12. Willard Ropes Trask, *The Unwritten Song*, vol. 1 (New York: Macmillan, 1966), p. 80. My first discussion of this song was in *The Reasons of the Heart*, p. 3.

13. "Voice" is one of the main topics in *Jazz Text* by Hartman. His subtitle is "Voice and Improvisation in Poetry, Jazz, and Song."

14. Hartman, *Jazz Text*, pp. 60–61 (jazz version) and p. 64 (vocal version).

15. Ibid., p. 70.

16. B. B. King quoted by Roger St. Pierre, *The Best of the Blues* (San Francisco: HarperCollins, 1993), p. 7.

17. John E. Abbey, editor of *Blues and Soul* magazine, quoted by Roger St. Pierre, *The Best of the Blues*, p. 21.

18. Ralph Tee, *The Best of Soul* (San Francisco: HarperCollins, 1993), p. 20.

19. Ibid., p. 28.

20. Ibid.

21. Max Jacob in his preface to *The Dice Cup*, his book of prose poems ed. by Michael Brownstein (Ithaca, N.Y.: State University of New York Press, 1979). See my discussion in *The House of Wisdom*, p. 111, and in *Love's Mind*, p. 77.

22. B. B. King quoted by Ralph Tee, *The Best of Soul*, p. 33. The idea is taken up by Stacy Harris, *The Best of Country* (San Francisco: HarperCollins, 1993), p. 6.

23. Henry David Thoreau, "Walking," in his *Natural History Essays* (Salt Lake City: Gibbs Smith, 1980), p. 94.

24. Goethe, *Faust*, Part 1, Studierzimmer, lines 1549–1550 (my trans.). I am using *Goethe's Faust*, ed. B-M. S. Haffner, Helmut Rehder, W. F. Twaddell (Boston: Heath, 1954), vol. 1, p. 213.

25. Stephen Leacock, *Nonsense Novels* (New York: Dodd, Mead, 1943), p. 60 (this novel is "Gertrude the Governess").

26. Hartman, *Jazz Text*, p. 10.

27. Ibid., p. 21.

28. Eric Clapton quoted by Alan Clayson, *The Best of Rock* (San Francisco: HarperCollins, 1993), p. 18.

29. See these titles in Paul Elliott and Jon Hotten, *The Best of Metal* (San Francisco: HarperCollins, 1993), pp. 7–9 and p. 13.

30. Hartman, *Jazz Text*, p. 9.

31. Bernard Lonergan, *Method in Theology* (New York: Herder & Herder, 1972), p. 290.

32. Ivan Nagel, *Autonomy and Mercy*, trans. Marion Faber and Ivan Nagel (Cambridge, Mass.: Harvard University Press, 1991).

33. "Act only according to that maxim whereby you can at the same time will that it should become a universal law." Immanuel Kant, *Grounding for the Metaphysics of Morals*, trans. James W. Ellington (Indianapolis and Cambridge: Hackett, 1981), p. 30.

34. *The Book of Common Prayer 1559*, ed. by John E. Booty (Charlottesville: University of Virginia Press, 1976), p. 291.

35. Ernst Cassirer, *The Philosophy of Symbolic Forms*, trans. Ralph Manheim (New Haven: Yale University Press, 1953–1957), vol. 1 *Language*, vol. 2 *Mythical Thought*, vol. 3 *The Phenomenology of Knowledge*.

36. Shakespeare, *The Merchant of Venice*, act 4, scene 1, lines 182–84, in *The Pelican Shakespeare*, ed. Alfred Harbage (Baltimore: Penguin, 1969), p. 236.

37. I am using the Breitkopf edition of the score: Mozart, *Ave Verum* (Wiesbaden: Breitkopf & Hartel, 1991). The translation is my own.

38. I am using the score of the plainsong *Ave Verum* in the *Liber Usualis* edited by the Benedictines of Solesmes (Tournai, Belgium: Desclee, 1950), p. 1856. "O dulcis! O pie! O fili Mariae!" is the wording of the last stanza (also "vero fluxit sanguine" in the third stanza) in F. J. E. Raby, *The Oxford Book of Medieval Latin Verse* (Oxford: Clarendon, 1959), p. 410 (#287), and this same wording is used in the *Ave Verum* of Josquin des Pres (see below, note 43) and in the *Ave Verum* of William Byrd (see below, note 56). Raby says the author of the verses is unknown but places the song "after 1300."

39. Tolkien, *The Lord of the Rings*, p. 138.

40. George Steiner, *Real Presences* (Chicago: University of Chicago Press, 1989).

41. Tolkien, *The Lord of the Rings*, p. 971.

42. See Heidegger, *The Concept of Time*, p. 11E.

43. Josquin des Pres, *Ave Verum Corpus*, ed. Frank Damrosch (Boston: Schirmer, 1926). This is the one we sang, I believe, and has only the first part, that is the first two stanzas. For the complete motet with all three parts, all five stanzas, see *Werken van Josquin Des Prez*, vol. 1, ed. A. Smijers (Amsterdam: G. Alsbach, 1922), pp. 48–50.

44. Igor Stravinsky, *Symphony of Psalms*, vocal score by his son Soulima (London: Boosey & Hawkes, 1948).

45. Psalms 38:13 and 14; 39:2, 3, 4; and 150 of the Latin Vulgate (my trans. here).

46. Nagel, *Autonomy and Mercy*, p. 6.

47. I have before me William Shakespeare, *Complete Songs from the Plays*, ed. Candace Ward (New York: Dover, 1993) and *Complete Sonnets* (New York: Dover, 1991).

48. Stravinsky, *Three Songs from William Shakespeare* (London: Boosey & Hawkes, 1954).

49. Messiaen, *The Technique of My Musical Language*, trans. John Satterfield (Paris: Alphonse Leduc, 1956), p. 21 and again on p. 63.

50. Ludwig Wittgenstein, *Tractatus Logico-Philosophicus*, trans. C. K. Ogden (London: Routledge & Kegan Paul, 1992), p. 185 (#6.4311).

51. *The Letters of Mozart and His Family*, trans. and ed. Emily Anderson, vol. 2 (New York: St. Martin's, 1966), p. 907.

52. John Webster, *The White Devil*, act 5, scene 4, line 128 in John Webster, *The Duchess of Malfi and The White Devil* (London: Bodley Head and New York: Dodd, Mead, 1930), p. 241.

53. Sophie Haibel's letter in *The Letters of Mozart and His Family*, vol. 2, p. 976.

54. "Death Is Awful" by Doc Reed and Vera Hall in Erik Sackheim, *The Blues Line* (Hopewell, N.J.: Ecco, 1993), p. 25.

55. Kant in his early essay *Of the Beautiful and the Sublime*, trans. Carl J. Friedrich, *The Philosophy of Kant* (New York: Random House, 1993), p. 4.

56. See Joseph Kerman, *The Masses and Motets of William Byrd* (Berkeley and Los Angeles: University of California Press, 1981), pp. 288–90. The score I am using is William Byrd, *Ave Verum*, ed. H. Clough-Leighter (Boston: Schirmer, 1929).

57. The score I am using is Anton Webern, *Funf Canons* (Opus 16) (Vienna: Universal Edition, 1984).

58. Heidegger, *The Concept of Time*, p. 11E.

59. Jaroslav Seifert, *Mozart in Prague*, trans. Paul Jagisch and Tom O'Grady (Iowa City: Spirit That Moves Us Press, 1985), # X (no page numbers).

60. Saint John of the Cross, *Spiritual Canticle*, trans. E. Allison Peers, in *The Works of St. John of the Cross*, vol. 2 (Westminster, Md.: Newman, 1953), p. 84. Saint John is using the Latin here of Psalm 101:8 (=Psalm 102:7 in KJ).

61. Messiaen, *Technique of My Musical Language*, p. 34.

62. Matthew 10:29–31 (KJ).

63. Alain Cavalier (writer and director), *Therese* (France: AFC Films, 1986).

64. Saint John of the Cross, loc. cit. above in note 60.

65. Thrasybulos Georgiades, *Music and Language*, trans. Marie Louise Gollner (Cambridge: Cambridge University Press, 1982), pp. 4–7.

66. 1 John 4:18 (KJ).

67. See my translation of these two poems in *Love's Mind*, pp. 98 and 100–101.

68. See the translation of Kant, *Of the Beautiful and the Sublime*, by John T. Goldthwait (Berkeley and Los Angeles: University of California Press, 1991), p. 48, note.

69. Tolkien, *The Lord of the Rings*, pp. 994–95.

70. My translation of "in inferno non est vera aeternitas sed magis tempus" in Saint Thomas Aquinas, *Summa Theologiae*

(Turin and Rome: Marietti, 1952), vol. 1, p. 44 (I, q. 10, a. 3 ad 2).

71. Messiaen, *Technique of My Musical Language*, p. 13.

72. Ibid., pp. 13 and 31.

The Road of the Union of Love with God

1. Tolkien, *The Lord of the Rings*, p. 87.

2. The phrase "the road of the union of love with God" occurs in the prologue of *Dark Night of the Soul* by Saint John of the Cross, trans. E. Allison Peers, p. 34. "The night of sense" is discussed in the First Book, pp. 36–90, and "the night of spirit" in the Second Book, pp. 91–193.

3. Broch, *The Death of Virgil*, pp. 250–51.

4. Ibid., p. 60.

5. Dunne, *Love's Mind*, p. 100.

6. Roland Barthes, *A Lover's Discourse*, trans. Richard Howard (New York: Hill & Wang, 1983), pp. 171–72.

7. Pascal, *Pensées*, #481 in Chevalier, ed., *Oeuvres Completes*, p. 1222 (my translation).

8. Barthes, *A Lover's Discourse*, p. 171.

9. Simone Weil, *Waiting for God*, trans. Emma Craufurd (New York: Harper & Row, 1973), p. 135. See my discussion in *The Peace of the Present*, pp. 61–70.

10. T. E. Lawrence, *Seven Pillars of Wisdom*, p. 364. See my discussion in *Reasons of the Heart*, p. 1.

11. Dunne, *Love's Mind*, pp. 100–101.

12. Barthes, *A Lover's Discourse*, p. 171.

13. I first reported this conversation in *The Church of the Poor Devil*, p. 71.

14. I believe this is a saying of Alfred Adler, but I have never been able to locate it in his writing.

15. Abraham Pais's biography of Einstein, *Subtle Is the Lord*, is named for this saying.

16. Grimm, *Dear Mili*. See my discussion above at the end of the chapter "Of Time and the Ecstasy of Being Ever."

17. Henryk Mikolaj Górecki, *Symphony No. 3* ("Symphony of Sorrowful Songs"), Opus 36 (London: Boosey & Hawkes, 1992), pp. 4 and 5 (music on pp. 32–46) (my translation).

18. See my discussion in *The House of Wisdom*, p. 36.

19. Barthes, *A Lover's Discourse*, p. 171.

20. See Arnold Schoenberg, *Self-Portrait*, ed. Nura Schoenberg Nono (Pacific Palisades: Belmont, 1988), pp. 119–23.

21. Patricia McKillip, *Something Rich and Strange* (New York: Bantam, 1994), p. 95.

22. Tolkien, *The Lord of the Rings*, p. 292.

23. Spinoza, *Ethics*, trans. G. H. R. Parkinson (London: Dent, 1989), p. 209 (*Ethics* V: 15), "rejoices accompanied with the idea of God."

24. Ibid., p. 208.

25. I Kings 3:5–9 (RSV).

26. Novalis as quoted by Etienne Gilson, *God and Philosophy* (New Haven: Yale University Press, 1941), p. 102.

27. See Tolkien's use of the phrase in *Smith of Wooton Major* (Boston: Houghton Mifflin, 1967), p. 36. See my discussion in *Love's Mind*, p. 10.

28. Barthes, *A Lover's Discourse*, p. 172.

29. John 1:14 and 1 John 1:1.

30. MacDonald, *The Golden Key*, p. 34 (also p. 45).

31. Ramon Lull, *The Book of the Lover and the Beloved*, trans. E. Allison Peers (London: SPCK, 1923), p. 49 (#118).

32. "Dionysius' Mystical Teaching" in *The Cloud of Unknowing and Other Works*, trans. Clifton Wolters, p. 209.

33. Broch, *The Death of Virgil*, p. 376.

34. Saint John of the Cross, *Dark Night of the Soul*, p. 95.

35. Lawrence, *Seven Pillars of Wisdom*, p. 364.

36. Broch, *The Death of Virgil*, p. 479.

37. Ibid., p. 439.

38. Heidegger, *The Concept of Time*, p. 12E.

39. Ibid., p. 13E.

40. Ibid., p. 12E.

41. Heidegger, *Being and Time*, p. 19 (time as horizon); Preface to William Richardson, *Heidegger: Through Phenomenology to Thought*, p. viii (his "turn around" or "reversal") and p. xx ("the lighting up of the self-concealing"). Compare Heidegger, *Discourse on Thinking*, p. 55, on "mystery" as "that which shows itself and at the same time withdraws." See my discussion in *The Homing Spirit*, p. 17.

42. Robertson Davies, *Fifth Business* (Toronto: Macmillan, 1970), p. 305. See my discussion in *The Homing Spirit*, p. 42.

43. Broch, *The Death of Virgil*, p. 480.

44. E. M. Forster, *Howards End* (New York: Random-Vintage, 1989), p. 32. See my discussion in *Love's Mind*, p. 43.

45. See "Lyric Theatre," next to last song.

46. Broch, *The Death of Virgil*, p. 481.

47. See above, "Of Time and the Ecstasy of Being Ever," note 48.

48. Pascal, *Pensées* #476 in Chevalier, ed., *Oeuvres Completes*, p. 1221 (my translation).

49. Tolkien, *The Lord of the Rings*, p. 439.

50. From *The Ascent of Mount Carmel* in *The Collected Works of Saint John of the Cross*, trans. Kieran Kavanaugh and Otilio Rodriguez (Washington, D.C.: Institute of Carmelite Studies, 1979), p. 97.

51. Tolkien, *The Lord of the Rings*, p. 427.

52. Pascal, *Pensées* #477 in Chevalier, ed., *Oeuvres Completes*, p. 1221 (my translation).

53. Plato, *Meno* 81 in Benjamin Jowett, trans., *The Dialogues of Plato* (New York: Random House, 1937), vol. 1, p. 360.

The Heart of Mystery

1. MacDonald, *The Golden Key*, p. 60.

2. Shakespeare, Sonnet 116, line 1 in William Shakespeare, *Complete Sonnets* (New York: Dover, 1991), p. 51.

3. George Steiner, *Martin Heidegger* (Chicago: University of Chicago, 1991), p. 158.

4. Ibid., pp. 15, 131, and 146.

5. Ibid., p. 158.

6. See my *Love's Mind*, p. 136.

7. Broch, *The Death of Virgil*, p. 43.

8. Proust, *On Reading*, p. 31 and p. 65.

9. Arvo Pärt, *Magnificat* (Vienna: Universal Edition, 1989).

10. A quotation from Basho (Zen Master) at the beginning of the program notes for Arvo Pärt's *Arbos* (Munich: ECM Records, 1987).

11. Herman Melville, *Moby Dick*, ed. by Alfred Kazin (Boston: Houghton Mifflin, 1956), p. 306 (chapter 88).

12. Lewis Shiner, *Deserted Cities of the Heart* (New York: Bantam, 1991).

13. Ursula LeGuin, *A Wizard of Earthsea* (Berkeley: Parnassus, 1968), p. 185. See my discussion in *The House of Wisdom*, p. 13.

14. Rilke, *Letters*, trans. Jane Bannard Greene and M. D. Herter Norton (New York: Norton, 1948), vol. 2, p. 157 (Letter to Imma Baroness von Ehrenfels, February 20, 1917).

15. Plotinus, *Enneads* 6:9 in A. H. Armstrong, trans., *Plotinus*, vol. 7 (Cambridge, Mass.: Harvard University Press, 1988), pp. 333 and 335.

16. Jean Giono, *The Man Who Planted Trees*, trans. and afterword by Norma L. Goodrich (Chelsea, Vt.: Chelsea Green, 1985), p. 51.

17. Tolkien, *The Lord of the Rings*, p. 292.

18. Ursula LeGuin, *A Fisherman of the Inland Sea* (New York: Harper Prism, 1994), p. 170 and p. 147.

19. Kathleen Norris, *Dakota*, p. 102.

20. Giono, *The Man Who Planted Trees*, p. 4 (original title when first published in *Vogue* in 1954).

21. Paul Celan, *Collected Prose*, trans. Rosmarie Waldrop (Manchester, U.K.: Carcanet, 1986), pp. 49–50.

22. Martin Buber, *I and Thou*, trans. Ronald Gregor Smith (New York: Scribner's, 1958), p. xv, and trans. Walter Kaufmann

(New York: Scribner's, 1970), p. 26. "So hab'ich endlich von dir er-harrt: In allen Elementen Gottes Gegenwart" from Goethe's *West-östlicher Divan*, ed. Hans-J. Weitz (Frankfurt am Main: Insel, 1979), p. 102.

23. Simone Weil, *Waiting for God*, trans. Emma Craufurd (New York: Harper & Row, 1973), pp. 68–69.

24. Psalm 88:18 (KJ).

25. R. M. French, trans., *The Way of a Pilgrim* (New York: Seabury, 1965).

26. Patricia McKillip, *The Sorceress and the Cygnet* (New York: Ace, 1991), p. 224.

27. Celan, *Collected Prose*, p. 49.

28. Patricia McKillip, *The Cygnet and the Firebird* (New York: Ace, 1993), p. 233.

29. Celan, *Collected Prose*, p. 49.

Index

abandonment, 30, 32, 95–96, 110

abyss between heart and heart, 68, 71, 73; time as, 71, 74, 79, 84, 197n20

Adorno, Theodor, 16–17

Aeneid (Virgil), 72, 79, 86, 88

air, in cycle of fire, 72–73, 75, 78

Alcmaeon, 84

"All One" (Dunne), 109–12, 113, 119, 121, 125

aloneness, x-xi, 26–29, 31–32, 46, 62, 155; as "all oneness," 123–25, 127; with the Alone, 28–29, 31–32, 64, 157–59, 164–65; in facing death, 110; with the human alone, 157–59; and solitude, 6, 44, 157; and spiritual friendship, 13–14, 26; and unaloneness, 2–3, 5, 6, 119, 123, 167; in way of music as a state of being, 97–105,

117. *See also* loneliness; walking alone

Alzheimer's disease, living with, 13

Andenken (thinking back), 4, 6, 49

"angel's cry, the," 77–80, 83

Aristotle, 103

Atman, 87

atonal music, 115, 116, 120

attention/attentiveness, as the natural prayer of the soul, 60–61, 65, 125, 161–62, 165, 168; all living creatures included in, 89–90; as a letting go, 58–59; music seen as, 95, 103–4; possessed by Kafka, 50–51

Augustine, Saint, viii, 13–14, 56, 85, 88, 126, 154, 156; *On Music*, 153, 156; *Soliloquies*, 48, 50, 52, 193n28. *See also Confessions*

categorical imperative, 106, 201n33

Caussade, Jean-Pierre de, 30

Celan, Paul, 161, 166, 168

chapels, 27, 28–29, 170

Chesterton, G. K., 32, 56–57

"Child's Way" (Dunne), 24, 190n37

choice, 20–21; freedom of, 106–7

Christ, 19, 50, 60, 85–87, 110, 121; Christ Within, 15–16, 25, 29, 58; real presence celebrated in *Ave Verum*, 107–9

Church of the Poor Devil, in Brazil, 27, 29, 170

"Church of the Poor Devil, The" (Dunne), xi–xii, 170, 171–77

Clapton, Eric, 101–2

Colemann, Ornette, 97–98

coming back. *See* passing over, and coming back

communication, 6, 156–58

communion, human, 26–32, 44, 155–59

companionship, vii–viii, x–xi, 9, 119, 166; and walking alone, 24, 29–30, 104–5, 151. *See also* friendship; human beings/humanity

Confessions (Augustine), 42, 44, 48, 50–51, 88–89, 164, 198n31; on coming from and returning to God, 37, 58

consciousness: of emergence and separation, 80–81, 83–85; in the Upanishads, 83, 85, 90

conversion, 94–95, 99

Corbusier, Le, 27, 29

counterpoint, in music, 112, 120

Country (music), x, 93, 94–95, 97, 99–100, 104–5, 164

Crumb, George, 18, 189n27

cycle of fire, 72–73, 75, 78, 80, 83

dance, 18, 115–16, 170; mystical, 126

Dance to the Music of Time, A (Powell), 185n1

Danken (thanking), unity with thinking sought by Heidegger, 153–54

Dante, 95–96

darkness: of longing, 40; of unknowing, 53–54

dark night of the soul, xi, 62. *See also* night of sense; night of spirit

Dark Night of the Soul (John of the Cross), 5, 125, 130–33, 136

Dasein (being there), 124, 145–46

Davies, Peter Maxwell, 37–38, 67

Davies, Robertson, 147

day of sense, 166

day of spirit, 166

Dear Mili (Grimm), 62–64, 65–66, 82, 134, 162, 195n55

oneness, 4, 76; in aloneness,
110–11; aloneness as,
123–25; with God, in the
Upanishads, 83, 85, 87, 90;
in way of music as symbolic
form, 117
On Music (Augustine), 153, 156

Pärt, Arvo, 157
Pascal, Blaise, 23, 132, 149, 151
passing over, xi, 5–6, 53, 196n13
and coming back, x, xi, 75–77,
99, 117; to Dante's hell, 96;
in encounters with other
persons, 9–10, 48, 155–57
"Patmos" (Hölderlin), 52–53
peace, 15, 20, 31–32, 86–87,
121–24, 146; coming to,
86–87; foretaste of in
Mozart's *Ave Verum*, 116–17;
found in being within the
story, 37–38; found in center
of stillness, 76–77
pentatonic scale, 84, 112
Pheney, Maura, xii, 171
plainsong, 17, 31, 108, 110, 112,
116, 201n38
Plato and Platonism, ix, 38, 151
Plotinus, 28, 159
poetry, viii, 13, 79, 90, 129,
167–68; first and second
voices of, 88; unity with
thought sought by
Heidegger, 153–54
Poizat, Michel, 77–78
polyphony, 111, 120
poverty: and prayer, 58; as
spiritual freedom, 60

Powell, Anthony, 185n1
prayer, x, 48–49, 51, 89–90, 160,
163–68; compared with storytelling, 65–66; as
contemplation of God, 60;
"heart speaks to heart" in,
19–20; interior soliloquy as,
46–48; "I walk alone" as a,
100, 164–65; of Kierkegaard
on longing, 34; longing in
loneliness becoming, 64–65,
161, 163; and poverty, 58;
relationship to fellow
humans as, 5, 45; as a state
of being and as symbolic
form, 164, 167. *See also*
attention/attentiveness
presence, 25, 36–37, 74, 119, 121,
123; as an answer to
loneliness, 108–11; of
Christ in the Eucharist,
107–8, 120–21. *See also*
Presence of God
Presence of God (the Shekinah),
6, 50, 74, 87, 135, 161; as an
answer to loneliness, 108–9,
165; experience of for John
of the Cross, 142; "I and
thou" relationship with,
163; living in the, 66, 138;
silence surrounding stillness
as, 77, 90, 158
present, the, living in, 36, 66
Proust, Marcel, 43–44, 157,
185n1
Psalms, 42, 154, 164; Stravinsky's
setting of, 111–12, 164
Psychedelic Rock (music), 101